THE EQUIPMENT OF THE US ARMY

US FIELD ARTILL
IN WORLD WAR
1941-45

PAUL GAUJAC

Colour plates by Nicolas GOHIN

Translated from the French by Roger BRANFILL-COOK

GW00771803

CONTENTS

I US FIELD ARTILLERY FROM WWI TO WWII   4

Up to the First World War   4
The lessons of the Great War   5
The reforms of the inter-war period   6
The situation on the eve
of the second worldwide conflict   7
The kick start of 1940-41   8
Large-scale maneuvers   9
Put on a war footing   10
Readjustments up until the close
of operations in Europe   10

II OPERATIONAL USE   12

"The finest artillery in the world"   12
Field artillery in action   13
Employment at divisional level   14
Employment at corps level   15
Fire direction and control   16
Ammunition   17
Liaison and observation   18
The field artillery observation battalion   19
Mobility   20

III THE ARTILLERY OF THE INFANTRY DIVISIONS   22

The infantry division   22
The "triangular" division   23
The manpower shortage   23
The divisional artillery headquarters   25
105 mm Howitzer M2A1, Carriage M2A2   26
The light direct support battalion   27

The medium general support battalion   28
Moves towards redeployment   30
155 mm Howitzer M1, Carriage M1A1   30
155 mm Howitzer M1918, Carriage M1918A3   33

IV THE ARTILLERY OF THE SPECIALIZED DIVISIONS   34

The experimental motorized divisions   34
A project cut short   35
The light divisions   36
Jeeps, mules and handcarts   37
The 71st and 89th Light Divisions   38
The 10th Mountain Division   39
By parachute and glider   40
The airborne divisions   41
Airborne artillery in action   42
75 mm Pack Howitzer M1A1, Carriages M1, M3 & M8   42
Artillery of the cavalry divisions   43

V THE ARTILLERY OF THE ARMORED DIVISIONS   46

The "Heavy" Armored Division   46
The "Light" Armored Division   47
The self-propelled 105 mm Battalion in 1943   48
105 mm Howitzer Motor, Carriage T19   49
105 mm Howitzer Motor, Carriage M7   50

VI LIGHT AND MEDIUM ARTILLERY OF THE GENERAL RESERVE

THE REFORMS OF 1943   2
Corps, brigades and groups   53
Field Artillery Battalions (75 mm Pack   54
Field Artillery Battalions (105 mm Howitzer)   55

Armored Field Artillery Battalions   56
4.5-inch Gun M1, Carriage M1A1   57
Field Artillery Battalions (155 mm Howitzer)   58

VII HEAVY ARTILLERY OF THE GENERAL RESERVE   60

Heavy Artillery problems   60
155 mm Gun M1, Carriage M1A1   62
Field Artillery Battalions (155 mm Gun)   64
Field Artillery Batt. (155 mm Gun, Self-propelled)   65
155 mm Gun Motor, Carriage M12   65
Field Artillery Battalions (8-inch Howitzer)   66
8-inch Howitzer M1, Carriage M1   66
Field Artillery Battalions (240 mm Howitzer)   68
240 mm Howitzer M1, Carriage M1   69
Field Artillery Battalions (8-inch Gun)   70
8-inch Gun M1, Carriage M2   71

VIII THE "AUXILIARY" ARTILLERY   72

Rocket Field Artillery Battalions (4.5-inch Rockets)   72
Chemical Battalions (Motorized)   73
Chemical Mortar Battalions   75
Infantry Cannon Companie   76
105 mm Howitzer M3, Carriages M3 & M3A1   77
Tank Destroyers   77
75 mm Howitzer Motor, Carriage T30   79
Tanks, Assault Guns and Antiaircraft Guns   80

IX CONCLUSIONS   81

X ACKNOWLEDGEMENTS & BIBLIOGRAPHY   82

Histoire & Collections - Paris

FIELD ARTILLERY FROM WORLD WAR I TO WORLD WAR II

Above.
The 105 mm Howitzer Motor Carriage T19
of the armored artillery battalions and the infantry
cannon companies saw action for the first time
in Tunisia in1943.

F OR LONG LINKED with the Coast Artillery and its air defense branch, the Field Artillery of the US Army comes second to the Infantry and before the Cavalry, in order of precedence.

While the French regard the Infantry as the "Queen of the Battlefield", for the US Army, Artillery remains the "King of Battle".

Ever since the War of Independence[1], and especially during the First World War, the US Artillery was influenced by French artillery, which greatly aided cooperation and a close relationship between the gunners of the two Allied armies.

UP TO THE FIRST WORLD WAR

During the siege of Boston in 1777, some sixty cannons captured from the British were collected together to form the first American artillery unit. Two years later, four regiments were in service, partly equipped with Gribeauval cannons left behind by Lafayette. However, by 1784 only one single battery was still in service, based at West Point.

In 1796, Congress decided to create the Artillery and Engineer Corps and steps were taken to ensure the training of officers, which in 1802, despite the fact that the two service arms had diverged in the meantime, resulted in the establishment of the United States Military Academy at West Point.

In 1816, letters of the alphabet designated the "companies" of the four active regiments. Then in 1861 the designation "battery" was used in the newly created fifth regiment. But it would take a further ten years before this designation became general in all units.

The Artillery School of the United States Army was established at Fort Monroe, Virginia. Closed between 1834 and 1856, during which period the Artillery participated in wars against Mexico and the Indian Tribes, it was reopened in 1856 only to close again at the start of the Civil War, being finally reformed in 1868. The distinctive emblem of the gunners during the latter conflict – scarlet stripes down the legs of their pants – gave rise to their nickname the "Red Legs".

In 1901 a new Corps of Artillery was created, bringing together the Coast and Field Artillery arms. The seven exis-

Tunic worn by a gunner of the Independent Field Artillery Brigade, with the patch of this unit sewn on the left sleeve. The two crossed cannons of the Field Artillery appear on the collar, on the left-hand side. (Le Poilu, Paris)

ting regiments were disbanded and the regimental scheme was abolished. Then in 1907, the two areas of specialization were completely separated to form two independent arms of service, the Coast Artillery Corps dealing with air and coastal defense, and the Field Artillery countering an enemy on land. Both arms however still kept their distinctive common color, the scarlet which can be seen on the flags and guidons of the various units as well as on the hat cords of the service and garrison caps. A dedicate school for the Field Artillery was set up at Fort Sill, Oklahoma, in 1911[2], while that for the Coast Artillery occupied Fort Monroe.

During the First World War, each of the infantry divisions – some fifty in total – included an artillery brigade of two regiments each with 24 guns[3] of 75 mm caliber, one regiment with 24 howitzers[4] of 155 mm caliber, and one battery of 12 trench mortars[5]. Of all the artillery pieces used in action, only 24 were of American manufacture. The French, who at that time had a major influence on the American Army, provided 3,834 guns and howitzers, and to serve these pieces the Americans were obliged to adopt the methods and procedures which their Allies had forged during the previous years of the War.

With the end of the War, the American gunners found themselves the possessors of a vast collection of equipment, of British, French and American origin. In addition, at home there were artillery pieces manufactured in the United States for foreign governments, but primarily of British design. There were several models of 75 mm and even naval guns of 240 mm caliber on tracked mountings. The first thing the gunners did was to place the guns of British design in reserve, for use in training.

The Army General Staff, being generally dissatisfied with the combat performance of the Artillery during the war, set up a commission of experts charged with designing and proposing a complete range of weapons to meet the needs of future conflicts. The Caliber or Westervelt Board, as it was known from the name of its president Brigadier General William I. Westervelt, started work in January 1919 and gathered reports of Allied artillerymen, studied German artillery pieces, and visited French armament factories.

Six months after its creation, the commission recommended a reduction in the number of calibers and different models, and suggested improvements to some existing pieces. It also proposed that a howitzer of 105 mm caliber should be adopted to accompany the 75.

THE LESSONS OF THE GREAT WAR

The projects for the majority of the artillery pieces produced during the 1930s, and also the concept of a complete "family" of related light, medium, heavy and super-heavy guns and howitzers, were the results of the experience gained in 1917 and 1918. First priority was to modernize the guns and howitzers supplied by the French, and then to progressively replace these with American designs better suited to the requirements of modern warfare.

The development of field artillery was centered on four basic types: a 75 mm pack howitzer, a 37 mm antitank gun, and howitzers in 105 mm and 240 mm caliber. A standard range of artillery pieces was finally perfected and the approved types went into production. The inter-war period was notable for the increase in the number of medium- and heavy-caliber weapons compared to those of lighter caliber, and also for the increased ranges achieved by all calibers.

Overall firepower was also increased. Drawing on the les-

sons of the combat operations of 1917-18, effort was expended on improving the ammunition. The need for greater range, accuracy and destructive effect led to a complete family of shells having increased fragmentation, velocity and penetrative capabilities. In addition, a range of fuzes was adopted which were interchangeable between virtually all shells.

Finally, a number of experiments were carried out into self-propelled mountings, towing characteristics and improved fire control facilities. The positive results of these experiments led to 61 out of the 100 batteries active in 1937 being motorized.

In parallel to the work of the Westervelt Board, in April 1919 a second commission made up of officers led by Major Gene-

The 151st FA Brigade, which was composed of the 301st, 302d and 303d Regiments took as its shoulder patch a black shell on a scarlet field, the distinctive color of the Artillery. (Le Poilu, Paris)

ral Joseph T. Dickman was charged with defining the future role and missions of the various combat arms, based on war experience.

They had to take into consideration the relative degree of mobility possessed by the largest caliber guns, and the feasibility of them following the Army in the field. The commission therefore stuck to traditional divides, and concluded that coastal defense artillery should retain its naval function but that mobile heavy artillery – whether towed or rail-borne – should revert to the control of the field artillery. For his part, the Chief of Coast Artillery, starting from the same basic premise, argued that the rationale behind separating the two arms of heavy artillery – the one on fixed platforms and the other capable of mobility – was invalid and that fusion of the two under his command remained feasible.

In the end, the new defense legislation passed in 1920 confirmed the separation of the heavy artillery. The legislation retained the possibility however, that in future, the President as head of the armed forces could decree the missions allocated to each arm of service.

This legislation also created the post of Chief of Field Artillery, which from 1 July 1920 was held by Major General William J. Snow[6]. This decision by Congress was followed in 1921 by an order from the War Department, defining the Field Artillery as the arm of service responsible for all the artillery to be used in land operations. Despite these moves, the controversy over control of the heaviest pieces would persist for several more years.

A 75 mm gun Model 1897 served by gunners of the AEF in France. The version of this gun manufactured in the USA would continue in service until 1940.

1-On 17 November 1775 Congress unanimously elected Henry Knox to be "Colonel of the Regiment of Artillery", theoretically established in January 1776.
2-The motto of the Field Artillery School - officially adopted on 21 Apr 19 – is "Cedat Fortuna Peritis" (Training removes the element of chance).
3-The gun has a long barrel compared to its caliber. It normally has a flat trajectory which eventually declines in a curve. Its range is greater than that of the howitzer or mortar of the same caliber.
4-The howitzer has a barrel of medium length compared to its caliber. It can fire at high-angle or flat trajectories but is optimized for the former. Its range is greater than the mortar but inferior to that of the gun.
5-The mortar has a short tube compared to its caliber. It uses only high-angle fire and its range is inferior to those of the gun and the howitzer.
6-Commanding Officer of the School of Fire of Field Artillery at Fort Sill with the rank of Colonel between 27 Jul and 26 Sep 17, and Major General between 26 Jun 18 and 19 Dec27.

(National Archives)

On 21 November 1942
during at the Army War
Show in Houston, Texas,
a battery of 75 mm Gun
Motor Carriage M3s
is giving a demonstration
of blank firing.

In 1927, the War Department stated that *"the combat mission of the field artillery is to assist the other arms of service, especially the infantry and the cavalry, with its firepower. It will include all the pack artillery, divisional artillery, corps artillery (excluding air defense), and the artillery of the General Reserve (excluding air defense and railway guns). Added to these are the sound locators and searchlight units supplied to the mobile army".*

The question of who should control the heavy artillery was once more brought up for discussion in April 1939, when the War Department planned economy measures. However, a quick study by the General Staff showed that the advantages of change would be minimal, and the status quo was retained.

THE REFORMS

OF THE INTER-WAR PERIOD

In terms of organization, the experience of the Great War called for three categories of field artillery: light, medium and heavy, used tactically by four different echelons: the division, corps, army and general reserve.

The divisional artillery would have to be mobile to accompany the infantry, and its primary target was the opposing infantry. The ideal weapon would have a barrel around 3-inch caliber, mounted on a chassis with 80 degrees elevation and all-round traverse. Firing a HE or shrapnel shell weighing around 20 pounds it should reach out to some 15,000 yards. The howitzer of 105 mm caliber would seem ideal, with an elevation of only 65 degrees, firing a shell weighing around 30 pounds to a maximum range of 12,000 yards.

The primary mission for the corps artillery was counter-battery fire, the secondary being harassing and interdiction fire along the whole front line. It would be made up of a brigade of two regiments armed with the 155 mm howitzer, one regiment of 155 mm guns, an observation battalion

equipped with sound locators and searchlights, and an ammunition train of five batteries. Its ideal weapons would be a gun of around five inch caliber, firing a 60 pound shell to a range of 17,500 yards, and a 155 mm howitzer firing a 100 pound shell out to 15,500 yards.

The army artillery would support the operations of the army and of the corps by calling on reinforcements drawn from the general reserve.

All categories of weapons would be represented in the general reserve. Its role would be to support the artillery components of the various echelons for the periods and the missions specified in the overall operational plan.

At maximum strength, it should comprise:

— six brigades, of three regiments of truck-mounted 75s each
— six brigades, of three regiments of towed 75s each
— six brigades, of three regiments of 155 guns plus two regiments of 240 howitzers each
— one regiment of 6-inch mortars and one regiment of 75 howitzers
— six observation battalions.

Ideally, it should be equipped with a 155 mm gun firing a shell of around 100 pounds to a maximum range of 24,000 yards and with an 8-inch howitzer firing a 230-pound shell to a maximum of 19,500 yards.

The majority of the artillery regiments were inactivated immediately following WW I, and no provision were made for their continuation, save in the case of mobilization. Fortunately, the defense legislation of 1920 was amended to allow the retention and continuation of the existing wartime units for as long as possible. As a result, several hundred field artillery units were reconstituted and attributed to the three components of the Army: the active Regular units, the National Guard and the Organized Reserve.

At the time it was planned to set up 90 battalions. In fact, only 12 complete and 10 incomplete regiments would form the light and medium Artillery of the Regular Army. There

Distinctive unit insignia
of the 1st Field Artillery
Battalion formed
in October 1940 from
the 1st Regiment of the 6th
Division. (Le Poilu, Paris)

was only one single heavy regiment, and in the event of mobilization, its four batteries of 155s and 240s would have to provide the core of over 30 Reserve regiments.

The National Guard, composed of civilian volunteers trained by each individual State along the lines laid down by the War Department, was to include 65 artillery regiments, attached primarily to the 22 divisions planned for the National Guard.

The 1920 legislation allowed for artillery regiments to be set up for the 29 Reserve divisions, but due to a lack of personnel (and in particular, officers), they existed on paper only.

The administration and the training of the forces based in the Continental United States were carried out by nine territorial commands. Then in 1932, at the instigation of General Douglas A. MacArthur[7], who had been Chief of Staff for two years, four Armies tasked primarily with organizing mobilization and running the four-yearly maneuvers headed the Corps Areas up.

THE SITUATION ON THE EVE OF THE SECOND WORLWIDE CONFLICT

Unfortunately, at the moment war broke out in Europe, the American Army ranked only seventeenth in the world, behind the Romanian Army. One section of the Regular

---

7-Army Chief of Staff, then Commanding Officer of the 84th Brigade and the 42d Infantry Division (10 Nov 18). West Point Academy Superintendent from 12 Jul 19 to 30 Jun 22.

Army – 42,000 men – was responsible for the occupation and defense of the overseas possessions, primarily the Hawaiian Islands, the Panama Canal Zone and the Philippines. The remainder – 134,000 men – served as trainers for the Regular Army active service officers and as instructors for the National Guard and the Reserve.

With a total of effectives equal to that of the Regular Army, the National Guard was organized by each State along the lines of a militia. In the event of a national crisis, by prior agreement of Congress it could be mobilized for Federal service. The Organized Reserves were composed of men – primarily officers – who had already seen a period of voluntary military service, and they essentially formed a pool of officers.

The overall structure included a certain number of incomplete and under-strength divisions. In the Regular Army there were three infantry divisions and one cavalry division based in the Continental United States, and three infantry divisions overseas. Eighteen infantry and four cavalry divisions were in the National Guard and twenty-seven infantry and six cavalry divisions in the Organized Reserves.

22,000 men strong, the infantry division had two brigades each with two infantry regiments, and one brigade of artillery comprising three regiments: two with three battalions of three batteries of 75s, and one with three battalions of two batteries of short-barreled 155s. The cavalry division of 10,000 men included two brigades each with two mounted regiments, and one artillery regiment with three battalions each with three batteries of 75s.

Collar badge worn by the Red Legs of the 90th Field Artillery Regiment from 1880 to 1900. One battalion of 155s bearing the same number was formed in October 1941 in the Hawaiian Islands with the 25th ID. (Le Poilu, Paris)

On 22 May 1944 in Washington, a 155 mm Howitzer M1 is displayed to the public. Its camouflage conforms to the field manual: olive drab and black, with undersides counter shaded in white to reduce shadows.

(National Archives)

On 3 August 1943, towed by an International M1 heavy artillery tractor, which was used by artillery units awaiting delivery of HSTs, a 155 Gun – probably from a battery of the 173d Battalion – comes ashore on the beach at Licata, Sicily.

Distinctive unit insignia of the 1st Infantry Division Artillery constituted in December 1941 and which, at the time included three battalions of 105s and one of 155s previously formed in October 1940. (Le Poilu, Paris)

Over and above these units, there were artillery elements not attached to any division, most only partially equipped, being:

18 regiments of 75 mm guns, of which 10 were motorized

— 5 regiments of 75 mm pack howitzers

— 6 regiments of motorized 155 mm howitzers

— 1 mixed motorized regiment armed with 155 mm guns and 240 mm howitzers

The Continental United States was divided up into nine Corps areas of which only two included active larger units of the Regular Army. They were grouped together into twos and threes to constitute four Army regions.

"For sure, this Army has not been inactive since 1918. But, for lack of sufficient funds, for lack also of that spur which is the realization of the approach of danger, there are a lot of questions needing answers, but few results have been achieved.[8]"

Among the outstanding questions was the formation of a Reserve for the Regular Army to comprise 75,000 men decided on in 1938 and to be completed by 1942, the reorganization of the regular divisions on the triangular basis tried out in 1937-38, and the introduction of new artillery pieces.

Placed third in order of priority behind the Navy and the Air Corps, the Army was reduced to a body of volunteers with limited means and operational capabilities. However, *"under the pressure of events, projects have been submitted to the American Congress to remedy these faults. But these projects are incomplete since, even if they aim to bring about a substantial increase in armaments and equipment, they do nothing to improve the manpower situation."*

In consequence, *"in the event of military action by the United States intended to support certain allied nations, American aid would not become effective until after long delays."*

THE KICK-START OF 1940-41

An initial emergency plan was drawn up in 1937-38, which aimed to mobilize 1,200,000 men, to be fully equipped and trained eight months after their call-up. But this ambitious plan depended on one pre-condition: the production and supply of the necessary equipment, which Congress deemed impossible. It would nonetheless serve as the starting point for the measures put in place between 1939 and 1942, which did not foresee the creation of any new units due to a lack of manpower.

On 8 September 1939, President Roosevelt proclaimed a limited State of National Emergency in order to reinforce national defense within peacetime financial limitations. General George C. Marshall, named one week later as Army Chief of Staff, immediately set to work to resuscitate the moribund Regular Army, using the increase in money and men voted by an increasingly anxious Congress.

In 1940, the traditional combat arms are Infantry, Cavalry, Field Artillery, Coast Defense Artillery, Air Corps, Engineer Corps and Signal Corps. This division of the various functions reflected the art of warfare as it existed in 1921, but rapid technological advances had produced new weapons and capabilities. Thus an appreciation of the military applications of aircraft had led to the creation of the Air Corps, and on land, mechanization had been the subject of continuous experimentation.

Each arm of service or traditional element was organized along the same institutional lines, with a school of the service arm and a committee. The school guaranteed the necessary professional training, established the operational doctrines and the instruction manuals, while the dedicated committee developed and tested the equipment.

The next development came on 26 July 1940, when the General Headquarters or GHQ was created under Brigadier

General Lesley J. McNair[9]. Its mission was to supervise the training of the four armies and nine corps established on the basis of the territorial areas, then to absorb into the Regular Army the units of the National Guard and the reservists.

Its first task was to learn from the lessons of the summer maneuvers, during which certain faults had come to light, notably the inadequate support of the infantrymen by their divisional artilleries.

The intervention of the GHQ became even more vital on September 16 when, following the fall of France, Congress authorized a selective increase in the manpower of the Army to a total of 1,400,000 men overall: 500,000 in the active Regular Army, 270,000 in the National Guard and 630,000 in the Reserve. The first concrete measure was the long over-due restructuring of the infantry division. Thus the old "square" structure adopted in 1917 during trench warfare in France was abandoned and replaced by the "triangular" system inhe-rited from the Germans, whereby one element maneuve-red under the protection of a second, while a third element was held in reserve.

On 1 October, nine infantry divisions of the Regular Army were reorganized along compound lines. As for the Field Artillery, the divisional regiments disappeared to be formed into autonomous battalions, the first of which would keep the number and the traditions of the parent body. The divi-sion would have at its disposal three light battalions of 105s, each being available for attachment to an individual infantry regiment, and a medium battalion of 155s dedicated to sup-port the whole division.

Overall, the restructuring aimed to maximize the latest developments in artillery equipment. Accurate fire, speed of reaction and flexibility came to replace simple volume of fire in the search for greater efficiency. Thanks to improvements in the means of signals, and to advances in the techniques of observation and fire control, the field artillery could hen-ceforward decentralize its batteries to significantly reduce their response time, while at the same time retaining their ability to call down massive firepower as and when required.

However, while they waited for the arrival of the 105 mm howitzer in 1941, the Field Artillery had to make the best of the 75s and 155s left over from the Great War.

LARGE-SCALE MANEUVERS

Relieved of its horses and of its non-essential services, the triangular division could field 15,000 men, which allowed for the creation of five new divisions in the place of every three in the former structure. All the new large units were then engaged in a series of large-scale war games concei-ved by General Marshall.

Also involved was an armored force made up of the two mechanized brigades activated by the Infantry and the Cavalry. These were to become the nucleus for the armored division which took its inspiration directly from the Panzer Division, but differed from the German model in that it initially was not possible to group together its elements into tactical units. Important features were an artillery regiment of two batta-lions attached to the armored brigade and one battalion at the level of the division.

A parallel development, first discussed in April 1941, was the creation of a powerful antitank arm to take account of lessons from the war in Europe. At first it was decided to form units equipped with artillery capable of antitank employ-ment, and to group them together as part of the General Reserve in order to engage armor en masse. Finally, all links with the Infantry and the Artillery were severed, and the Tank Destroyer Forces became independent.

In other directions, in order to activate an airborne force, from July 1941 onwards experiments were conducted into the transport of men and equipment in gliders, with the aim of being able to deploy a tactical airborne unit of infantry battalion size, plus an antitank company and an artillery bat-tery. The trial parachute drops of the 75 mm pack howit-zer carried out at the same time would lead to the creation of the first battery in March 1942[10].

During the summer of 1942, the planned target of 1,400,000 men was close to being attained. The Army based in the Continental United States was now in the throes of restructuring, and four armies with nine corps, comman-ding 31 divisions, would be available in short order. This growth in manpower had come about through pressure of events. As a pre-condition General Marshall – much like his counterpart in the Navy - had insisted upon an increase in ammunition production. However, the situation with regard to equipment and armament was far from satisfactory, the

more so because President Roosevelt had made the deci-sion to aid Great Britain, which was on its knees, to the detri-ment of his own army.

The large-scale maneuvers carried out in Louisiana in September, then in the Carolinas in November, brought to a close the reorganization phase of the Army. Involved in these maneuvers in part or in whole were: three army and eight corps headquarters, the four armored and cavalry divi-sions, six "triangular" infantry divisions of the Regular Army and sixteen out of eighteen divisions of the National Guard (still organized along "square" lines), plus four artillery briga-des and an observation squadron. In fact for these war games the Artillery used the new 105 mm howitzer and eleven light aircraft loaned by their civilian manufacturers.

Driven by the impetus of General McNair, charged with training the Army, the large-scale war games allowed the individual units to acquire experience of combined arms ope-rations, which was impossible to pick up in the confines of the training camps. They met the requirements of General Marshall, chief of all ground forces, who preferred that any errors be made during the training exercises, rather than in combat.

Embroidered patch of the Field Artillery School, inspired by its distinctive metal insignia, worn during the war but officially approved only at its end. (Le Poilu, Paris)

A Piper L-4B Cub of the II Corps air observation school flies over a 105 mm Howitzer M2A1 battery of the 29th Infantry Division during an exercise near Tidworth, England, in March 1943.

8-Information bulletin dated March-April 1939 from the Army General Staff G-2.

9-Commanding Officer of the Army Command and General Staff College at Fort Leavenworth, Kansas, from April 1939 to October 1940, Chief of Staff of the Army GHQ from 9 Jul 40 to 8 Mar 42 then Commanding Officer of the Army Ground Forces from 16 Jul 44.

10-The Chief of Artillery was charged with its organization, but the Chief of Infantry was responsible for training the airborne elements and the Chief of Ord-nance provided the guns.

Shoulder patch of the Army Ground Forces (AGF) created in March 1942 to replace GHQ. The armbands worn by General Pershing's staff officers during the First World War inspired the design. (Private collection)

A self-propelled 105 mm M7 of the 4th Armored Division during the relief of Bastogne in January 1945. Thanks to the censor, the only marking left on the machine gun ring mount indicates that this is vehicle #12 of Battery C.

During the period of semi-mobilization which began with the invasion of Poland and ended with the attack on Pearl Harbor, Army manpower was multiplied by a factor of eight, thanks to the influx of reservists and conscripts, and thirty-three divisions were raised - of which several were already fully operational - and the Field Artillery had doubled the number of its battalions to 80, compared with the previous period.

PUT IN WAR FOOTING

On 7 December 1941, the Japanese attacked the American base at Pearl Harbor, on Hawaii. On the following day, they landed in the Philippines, and four months later, the American forces in the Philippines were forced to surrender.

Further South, 17,500 men of the National Guard were sent to Australia where they arrived on 26 February 1942 before reaching Noumea on 12 March to join in the defense of New Caledonia. Among their ranks were two artillery battalions of National Guard regiments from Illinois and Massachusetts.

Then in the course of the first six months of the war, eight armored divisions, thirty-two infantry divisions and one airborne division completed their training and were readied for eventual deployment overseas.

Finally, during the period 1940 to 1943, the six 1939 divisions of the Regular Army were swelled by a further 86 divisions, of which more than half arrived during 1942. These new units were activated or, as regards the National Guard, called up for Federal service, as per the following table:

| | Infantry and Cavalry | | | Amd | Abn | Total |
	Regular	NG	Reserve			
1940	3	10	-	2	-	15
1941	3	9	-	3	-	15
1942	-	1	37	9	2	49
1943	2	-	-	2	3	7
Total	8	20	37	16	5	86

On 31 March 1945, 665 field artillery battalions had been formed. According to their means of transport, they were designated "HD" (horse-drawn), "Trk-D" (truck-Drawn), "Trac-D" (tractor-Drawn) or "S-P" (self-propelled).

Lastly, the battalions forming the artillery of the armored divisions were designated as "armored", and those of the airborne divisions were designated as "parachute" or "glider" according to their means of delivery.

To face up to the enormous demands for training, the Replacement and School Command was created to supervise all the training activities of the ground forces. For example, the School of Artillery at Fort Sill was placed under its control in March 1942. From an initial total of six courses offered at the outset, the number of courses rose to thirty-five, including in particular the courses leading to the diplomas of the USMA and the ROTC[11]. In addition, by 1945 26,000 officers had risen from the ranks, by means of the special program of the OCS[12] begun in July 1941. Finally, in August 1942 the first courses for the pilots of light observation aircraft began, with the aim of providing two planes per artillery battalion.

In parallel, three[13] of the Replacement Training Centers functioning by July 1942 carried out the basic training of young artillery recruits plus their technical and tactical instruction, so that they might reinforce an existing unit or help to establish a new one.

These activities were formalized in the new organization adopted on 9 March 1942, which aimed at rationalizing and optimizing the selection, equipping, training and deployment of the rapidly expanding ground forces. Its task fulfilled, the GHQ was in fact dissolved and three autonomous commands were established and placed under the control of General Marshall:

— Army Ground Forces or AGF

— Army Air Forces or AAF

— Army Service Forces or ASF, previously designated the Services of Supply.

Their authority was exercised only in the Continental United States, all forces engaged in operations remaining under the control of the War Department General Staff.

The constitution of the AGF under General McNair involved the suppression of the posts of the branch chiefs. One of those involved was Major General Robert M. Danford, Chief of Artillery since 26 March 1938. He had played a critical role in renovating the Field Artillery, including its reorganization and re-equipment with modern weapons.

READJUSTMENTS UP UNTIL THE CLOSE OF OPERATIONS IN EUROPE

One other general revision, planned by McNair and put into effect in July 1943, had a direct effect on the Field Artillery. The system of "type" army "type" corps adopted a year earlier was abandoned. The army retained their tactical and administrative role, but the corps was transformed into a balanced and flexible force in which a variable number of divisions were supported by an appropriate complement of artillery, mechanized cavalry, combat engineer, tank, tank destroyer and antiaircraft units, each organized into battalions and groups.

As for manpower, the target of 7,700,000 men set two years earlier was reached in May 1945, by the time operations in Europe ended.

Less than half of these troops were employed in ground combat formations. In addition, 500,000 were currently

(National Archives)

hospitalized, of whom 100,000 were scheduled either for demobilization or for returning overseas as replacements.

However, the supply of trained manpower was not inexhaustible, and on several occasions General McNair[14], in his role as Commanding General of the AGF, was obliged to order drastic reductions in the training of artillerymen, through whose ranks he himself had risen. In particular, in March 1943 the strength of the infantry 2,000 men, divided almost equally between the three infantry regiments and artillery, reduced division. But this reduction – essentially at command and support levels - had little effect on the batteries in the front line which retained the same number of artillery pieces.

At the same time, he sought to compensate for the imbalances caused by mobilization. It had become apparent that less antitank and antiaircraft units were actually required, while more battalions of heavy artillery would be advantageous.

Again, on several occasions between September 1942 and March 1944 the AGF recommended an increase in the artillery committed to the General Reserve – up to 101 medium battalions and in particular 140 heavy battalions – in order to constitute a more balanced force. Each time, the War Department cut back the requests, finally in July 1943 authorizing the deployment of first 77, then 111, heavy battalions[15]. Then in March 1944, the commission charged with evaluating artillery requirements recorded that, during the operations in the Monte Cassino sector, aerial bombardment could not satisfactorily replace heavy artillery. As a result, General McNair proposed a new increase in the number of heavy battalions, mostly combining 8-inch and 240 mm pieces. In the event authorization was granted for more heavy battalions than he had asked for, in fact more battalions than had been included in the previous ambitious requests from the AGF.

	Europe	Medit.	Pacific	Total
75 Pack How	4	-	3	7
105 How	36	1	8	45
S-P 105 How	16	2	3	21
155 How	73	7	16	96
4.5-inch Gun	16	-	-	16
155 Gun	31	4	8	43
S-P 155 Gu	6	-	-	6
8-inch How	37	2	7	46
8-inch Gun	5	-	1	6
240 How	15	-	5	20
Rocket	-	-	2	2
Total	239	16	53	308

339 light and medium battalions - around one half of the battalions formed during the course of the war - were incorporated in the divisions.

The other half – 76 light, 113 medium and 137 heavy battalions – belonged to the General Reserve.

This unprecedented growth was finally made possible through absorption of personnel from arms of service being run down, and by retraining Coast Artillery gunners[16].

The progress made by 8 May 1945, when combat ceased in Europe and when more than 300 artillery battalions were deployed in the various theaters of operation, can be measured as above:

The efforts of the Field Artillery had been prodigious. In four years of war they suffered over 36,000 casualties[17], 66 battalions were decorated with the Presidential Unit Citation for extraordinary heroism and 242 received a foreign decoration.

A battery of 105 mm Howitzers M2 of the 36th Infantry Division supports the troops carrying out an opposed crossing of the Moselle downstream from Remiremont on 21 September 1944.

11-Offered by 52 colleges and universities.
12-The Officer Candidate Schools were set up for officer candidates raised from the ranks.
13-At Fort Bragg in North Carolina, Fort Sill in Oklahoma and Camp Roberts in California, with a capacity of 25,000 trainees.
14-Having taken over as Commanding Officer of the First Army Group (Phantom) in England, he would be killed on 25 Jul 44 by friendly fire when observing the aerial bombardment leading up to Operation Cobra in Normandy.
15-Only 61 would have been activated by 1 Jan 44.
16-On the other hand, the production of sufficient artillery pieces and ammunition caused problems, which were never satisfactorily resolved.
17-36,140 gunners to be exact, of whom 8,749 were killed or died of their wounds, 27,391 were wounded, and 7,013 were taken prisoner or listed as missing.

(National Archives)

A 155 mm Howitzer
M1918 in action inside
the Anzio beachhead
in May 1944

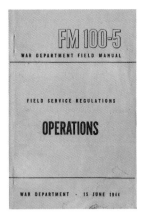

FM 100-5
WAR DEPARTMENT FIELD MANUAL

FIELD SERVICE REGULATIONS

OPERATIONS

WAR DEPARTMENT · 15 JUNE 1944

*Field Service Regulations,
Operations, the version of the
manual issued on 15 June
1944 incorporating the
changes shown necessary by
the operations in Tunisia,
Sicily and Southern Italy.
(Private Collection)*

OPERATIONAL USE

*" A s regards the ordnance, our artil-
lery is the best in the world. Our
signals network is probably also
quite remarkable.*

*The tactical and technical doctrines as perfected by the
Artillery School and then put into c in the various operational theaters have always proved themselves to be correct at the moment of combat. However, the possession
of excellent arms, the perfecting of the means of message
signalling, and a remarkable system of fire control, do not
in themselves guarantee effective support at the critical
moment in the course of a battle. The more intangible
questions of organization, of coordination, of esprit de
corps and of morale are of equal if not greater signifi-
cance.[1]"*

"THE BEST ARTILLERY IN THE WORLD"

Learning from the lessons of the Great War, the US Field
Artillery concentrated during the inter-war period on obtaining new weapons, which would come into their own between 1942 and 1945. Under the impetus of the Westervelt
Board a range of towed artillery pieces was designed, in four
basic categories - light, medium, heavy and super-heavy –
most of which included a long-barreled gun alongside a short-
barreled howitzer mounted on carriages which were for all

intents and purposes identical.

Five howitzers and two guns came to comprise the basic
armament of the field artillery:

— 105 mm Howitzer M2, very effective against personnel in the open or with scant protection, capable of destroying
light field breastworks, automatic weapons or antitank guns,
barriers and lightweight obstacles

— Self-propelled 105 mm Howitzer M7 with the same
capabilities, but used in support of armor[2]

— 55 mm Howitzer, a powerful weapon, used for barrage fire, for destroying entrenchments, buildings and mode-
rately dug-in gun batteries, capable of killing or neutralizing
personnel in defile and dug in, notable for its high angle capability and its wide field of traverse

— 155 mm Gun, having the same destructive capabilities
as the howitzer of the same caliber, but with a longer range,
reserved for long-distance action, harassing and interdiction
or counter-battery work

— 8-inch Howitzer, a powerful destructive arm for firing
against solid bunkers, casemates, villages

— 8-inch Gun and 240 mm Howitzer, both employed
either for long range destructive fire against enemy communications or fortification lines, or for counter-battery work.

Despite being usually excellent and robust, these weapons
however would not suffice on their own. Other elements
came into play: motorization first and foremost, which affected the whole of the US Army. Except for several pack ani-

mal units, the Artillery was totally motorized, which allowed it to fully participate in combined arms combat operations. The robust nature of the vast range of suitable vehicles, played a critical role both tactically and logistically. But the most significant of the special support functions was the centralized Fire Direction Center, coupled with air observation and signal transmissions. The ammunition obviously played a key role, a primordial one in fact - due basically to the wide range of propellant charges and the precision of the fuzes – in as much as they formed a coherent, homogenous system supported by an efficient supply chain.

Although the US Field Artillery's operational doctrine closely resembled that of other armies, what at the end of the day set it apart, and ensured its superiority, was the widespread use of radio and dedicated artillery observation light aircraft, which dramatically modified its operational employment - as the French Army was to discover when it was being rearmed by the Americans in 1943.

Tactical and logistical maneuvers became possible thanks to the "motor" element, the link between them being the "radio". The "motor" facilitated rapid movement and the "radio" coordinated that movement with the deployment of the other arms, notably the armored units. Thanks to real-time information and aerial observation, a large number of shells could be placed in exactly the right place with a maximum of efficiency and speed.

According to the regulations, *"Field Artillery contributes to the action of the entire force through the fire support which it renders other arms. It has two principal missions in combat*

— It supports Infantry (Cavalry, Armored) units by fire, neutralizing or destroying those targets which are most dangerous to the supported arms

— It gives depth to combat by counter-battery fire, by fire on hostile reserves, by restricting movement in rear areas, and by disrupting hostile command agencies" [3].

The raison d'être of the field artillery was its ability to support the infantry on the battlefield. Its overall employment – including that of the heavy artillery – was linked to the deployments planned for the infantry. As a result, *"the Direct Support Battalion is the cornerstone of the entire organization of the Artillery".*

FIELD ARTILLERY IN ACTION

Despite the fact that in Tunisia, apart from sharp reverses at the Kasserine Pass and Fondouk, the raw American troops had conducted themselves rather well, coordination between the various arms of service had fallen down. Some infantry battalions had not followed up the artillery preparation, allowing the enemy to re-establish his defense, and sometimes the artillery had lifted its fire too soon after an objective had been taken, allowing the enemy to immediately counterattack and regain the position.

Attacks launched in the last hours before dawn were advantageous for the infantrymen, but caused problems for the gunners. Night movements were more difficult for them because of their heavier equipment and the time required to set up their new positions. In order to reduce the risks of being detected, they tended to rush changes of position to the detriment of defensive measures. As a result, if the enemy counter-attacked at the wrong moment the howitzers could fall into their hands before machine guns had been put in position to cover the approaches.

During the Sicilian campaign and in the initial phase of the

(National Archives)

Chest insignia worn by the personnel of the Department of Light Aviation at Fort Sill Training Center. (M. Pleissinger/H & C)

campaign in Italy, the field artillery was employed within the regiment combat teams. This solution worked well for landing operations, and for moving against an enemy which was not using prepared defensive positions.

Towards the end of 1943, and in very different conditions, the Americans adopted an arrangement which allowed both for continual support of the troops, and for varying the concentration of firepower according to the situation. As for the corps artillery, even if there existed "unofficial ad hoc units" capable of intervening in the zones of one division or another, the corps artillery was essentially employed "en masse" and in "large packets", of which the composition varied to suit the specific operation, and which also sucked in the divisional artillery.

This technique was feasible because of an abundance of artillery pieces and ammunition, and also because of the training of the officers, who were more prepared to use their equipment in new theoretical ways instead of relying on the old traditional procedures.

In order to ease the tasks of subordinate echelons, an exclusive feature was the set-piece barrage, laying down concentrations of firepower from a large number of battalions over a vast zone. According to statements obtained

From enemy prisoners, the high ammunition consumption, which resulted, was often out of all proportion to the results obtained and to the number of infantrymen engaged in the operations.

The gunners tended to occupy positions which in peacetime would have been judged untenable. Emplacing the howitzers was usually carried out at night, but the camouflage of the positions was all-too-often inadequate. The large number of rounds fired each day by the units from their prepared positions enabled the enemy to quickly spot their location.

In Naples on 4 October 1943, a Piper L-4 carrying Lieutenant General Clark, commander of the Fifth Army, takes off from the Via Caracciolo guarded by the paratroops of the 509th Battalion

Distinctive unit insignia of the 2d FA Battalion formed at the end of 1940 in the Canal Zone. The pack mule carrying a 75 recalls the specialization of the 2d (Mountain) Regiment. (Le Poilu, Paris

---

1-Brigadier General W. Lee Hart, Artillery Officer of the II Corps in Tunisia and Sicily, then of the First Army in Europe.
2-However, the fact that it was self-propelled meant that the howitzer depended on the continued mobility of the motorized component to which it was attached.
3-Field Manual 100-5 Operations 15 June 1944, Chapter 2, Paragraph 42.

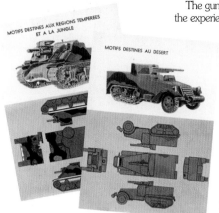

Extracts from the Field Manual 5-20B (French), Vehicle Camouflage, circulated by the Engineer Corps in July 1944, showing a 75 mm M3 in "desert" camouflage and a 105 mm M7 in "temperate regions and jungle" colors. (Private Collection)

The six self-propelled Howitzers M7 of Battery B of the 22d Armored FA Battalion of the 4thArmored Division before leaving for England in December 1943

The gunners who later fought in France benefited from the experience of combat in Italy through the efforts of the Artillery School. The next potential problem area was the heavy artillery, where the number of battalions was expanding rapidly, but this was avoided thanks to the excellent training received by all ranks at Fort Sill. However, the armored artillery – 105s and 155s – was where lessons were still to be learned, for the single force armed with these weapons was confined to Italy with the 1st Armored Division.

Two basic factors gave the artillery of an armored division its high degree of effectiveness:

Firstly it had impressive firepower because of its large number of howitzers and guns, typically fifty four 105 mm howitzers plus nine observation tanks armed with 75 mm guns, in some cases reinforced by tank destroyers and gun tanks; secondly, the abundance of its radio equipment which allowed for a rapid concentration of fire.

A further factor was the flexibility brought about by the mobility of its pieces, by its armor protection allowing deployment in advanced positions, and once again the value of its radio communications which allowed for rapid redeployment to meet changing combat situations.

When exploitation proceeded in leaps and bounds, the armored artillery became largely decentralized. Each battalion of 105s operated under the control of its own combat command. At corps level, one battalion could be attached to a mechanized cavalry element on long range reconnaissance[4]. When exploitation was patchy, or the division was slowed or even halted all along the front, maximum firepower could be concentrated to force a breakthrough. Finally, concentration

when on the defensive – as well as the use of free-ranging units to add volume of fire, or thwart enemy counter-battery fire – was also necessary where the defenses were spread thinly.

EMPLOYMENT AT DIVISIONAL LEVEL

The divisional artillery (DA) included a command body, organic battalions and, as the need arose, "attached" units, in other words, units placed under the orders of the commanding general of the divisional artillery on a temporary basis[5]. The organic divisional artillery represented the minimum artillery force which could support a division encountering weak opposition.

The command structure of the divisional artillery was centralized when the battalions could act in concert and when communications were good. In such circumstances, concentrations of firepower could be easily effected. On the other hand, the command would be decentralized when the division was spread out over a wide front or when communications were difficult. In this case, the commanding officer of the divisional artillery had to be ready at any moment to reassert overall control of his individual battalions.

Units were attached according to the operations planned for the infantry. Each light battalion[6] would generally be placed as direct support for the same infantry regiment. When battalions were joined together into support groups, it would be the commanding officer of the battalion normally attached to the infantry regiment concerned who would take overall command of this combined force.

When an infantry regiment was not in action, its usual direct support battalion could be attached to the general support group, but its liaison detachments remained alongside their own infantry units, so that if the need arose the batta-

lion could intervene without delay in support of its own infantry. The sole divisional medium battalion[7] was used in combined fire support, but was usually directed to reinforce the firepower of an individual direct support battalion.

A divisional artillery could use "attached" units such as artillery battalions and observation batteries. In addition, certain battalions of the corps could be allocated to reinforce the firepower of the divisional artillery. In the final analysis of the campaign in Europe, it was held that reinforcement as and when required was preferable to permanent integration. Nevertheless, in his report drafted in December 1945, General Hart – as reported elsewhere by his French counterparts – recommended that a battalion of towed or self-propelled 155 mm howitzers be included as an integral part of each infantry or armored division.

The divisional artillery commanding general coordinated the work of all the observation units other than the forward observers. His control oversight also allowed him to share other observers when his own division's spotters were thinly spread.

He acted as the technical adviser to the general commanding the division, in which capacity he could continually update the latter as to the potential of his artillery units and proffer suggestions for their use. Once a course of action had been decided, he drafted the paragraph dealing with the role of the artillery in the operational orders, and was responsible for preparing the detailed action plan in the annex dedicated to artillery.

He had at his disposal a deputy and a staff of six officers:
— S-1 for administrative matters
— S-2 for intelligence, with one of his officers dealing with reconnaissance and topography
— S-3, charged with drawing up the orders and matters of deployment, notably the establishment of the fire plan
— S-4 for ammunition supply
— signal officer, who also commanded the HQ battery
— chief of the air observation post, who doubled as the technical adviser to the divisional artillery staff.

What was noted above in respect of the artillery of an infantry division held good for the armored division as well, except that the latter had no medium battalion. However, the desirability of including a battalion of self-propelled 155s continued to feature in reports.

EMPLOYMENT AT CORPS LEVEL

The mission of the corps artillery was to further the aims of the corps by reinforcing the firepower of the divisional artillery, by neutralizing or destroying the opposing artillery, by attacking enemy reserves, communications and command posts.

Compared with the DA, the only units integral to the corps artillery were the staff and the field observation battalion. The battalions coming under its direct control were allocated to the corps artillery out of the General Reserve.

The battalions were generally joined together in groups with a specific mission, normally to reinforce the divisional artillery units. The field observation battalion, in addition to its mission to locate enemy batteries, participated in general observation activities and drew up maps of the local topography.

The command structure of the corps artillery was basically similar to that of the DA. Its responsibilities were wider in scope, and therefore its staff was larger. A single officer handled the lesser duties of the S-1, but the duties of the S-2 were shared between several. One of these was charged with counter-battery work, a second liaised with the Corps G-2, and a

(National Archives)

third was permanently seconded to the PC of the tactical air forces where he worked closely with the photographic reconnaissance section. The S-3 section was also expanded, with an officer specializing in counter-battery fire and a liaison officer for each of the divisional artillery.

When the Third Army readied itself to break through the German lines in Normandy in August 1944, the overall mission given to the artillery units attached to each corps was to "aggressively support the attack with all available forces" [8]. To achieve this end the non-divisional units were allocated in support as follows:

As regards each army, there were, properly speaking, no artillery units regularly attached to these formations, apart from an artillery section of the headquarters staff tasked with ensuring that each corps received the correct quota of men and equipment for each operation.

Operational experience showed however that units not normally included on the strength of a division should carry out the fire support for a corps, composed of three infantry divisions and one armored division. These could be designated exclusively for the support of the corps in question, or could initially remain under the control of the army to be exclusively attached at a later date according to the circumstances as above:

During most of the operations in Europe, First Army headquarters used the 33d Brigade as intermediary to control all the artillery units equipped with 8-inch and 240 mm pieces. Using this organisational setup, it could either concentrate all the firepower of its long-range artillery to support the corps at the head of the advance, or divide its firepower to rein-

In action in the Vosges, the 155 mm Howitzer M1 was "the most impressive artillery piece deployed in the sector", according to contemporary reports. Compared to the efforts of the Army Air Force, the support provided to attacking infantry by their artillery was the deciding factor.

4-In particular, this was the experience of the 4th Cavalry Group who in September 1944 reconnoitered ahead of XII Corps in the direction of Luneville. Meeting an enemy column, the troopers attacked frontally while their artillery bombarded the enemy rear, destroying 36 vehicles and causing heavy losses.
5-The "attached" units did not become an integral part of the division, but were simply made available and completely subordinated to its control.
6-In other words, equipped with 75 mm and 105 mm howitzers.
7-Equipped with 155 mm howitzers.
8-Annexe #2 to the Operational Order #1 dated 1 Aug44.

	VIII	8 ID	79 ID	4 AD	6 AD	XV	83 ID	90 ID	XX
Groups	2	1	1	1	-	4	-	-	1
105 towed	-	1	-	-	-	-	1	1	-
105 S-P	-	-	-	2	1	1	-	-	3
155 How	1	1	2	1	-	5	-	-	1
155 gun	1	1	1	-	-	3	-	-	-
155 gun S-P	1	-	-	-	-	-	-	-	-
8-inch How	1	-	-	-	-	1	-	-	-
Total	4	3	3	3	1	10	1	1	4

On 31 July 1944, near Carentan,
an 8-inch howitzer of the First Army.
Nicknamed "Berlin Buster", it is towed by an 18-ton HST M4.

(National Archives)

Non-Divisional Unit	Attached to the Corps	Remaining under Army control
Field Observation Bn	1	1
Brigade with HQ battery	-	1
Group with HQ battery	4	2
Towed 105 How Bn	2	-
S-P 105 How Bn	1	-
Towed 155 mm How Bn	3	-
S-P 155 mm How Bn	2	-
Towed 155 mm Gun Bn	2	-
S-P 155 mm Gun Bn	1	-
Towed 8-inch How Bn	1	1
S-P 8-inch Gun Bn	1	1
Towed 240 mm How Bn	-	3
S-P 240 mm How Bn	-	1

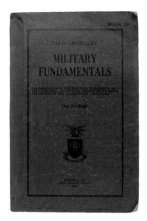

A manual of "Military
Fundamentals" prepared
by the Field Artillery
School and issued
in 1942 solely to military
personnel.
(Private Collection)

force the artillery of several corps. The artillery section of each army included some sixty personnel, with up to sixteen officers divided into five sub-sections each commanded by a Lieutenant-colonel or a major: S-2 (three officers), S-3 (four officers), antitank (two officers), air observation (three officers), S-4 (four officers).

FIRE DIRECTION AND CONTROL

Each battalion, irrespective of the caliber of its weapons, was composed of three firing batteries and a command element with a Fire Direction Center. Usually sited within the artillery CP, the FDC directed the "fire maneuver" which was the tactical command of one or more artillery units, in order to bring down their fire on the target at the required moment with the maximum density and the element of surprise.

Each FDC was connected by radio or telephone line with the ground or air observers whose role was to direct and correct the artillery fire. It used a system of firing table and graphic slide rule adapted for each caliber and type of piece.

The graph system was intended to simplify calculations of the firing solutions, previously the preserve of specially trained analysts. During the 1920s and 1930s, firing tables were drawn up to ease the preparation process and make up for the shortage of trained specialists. One continuing problem was that range calculations still required the input of a specialist.

Then in 1940, Captain Abbott H. Burns, a National Guard officer and qualified mathematician, was called to active service in the Regular Army and found himself attached to the Artillery, with the role of calculating firing tables. Finding the work tiresome and unrewarding, he improved on a civilian slide rule and invented the Graphical Firing Table or GFT. With the range and the bearing provided by the GFT and the firing tables, the calculations were simplified: without the need for highly qualified analysts, the work was done in one twentieth of the time, and accuracy was greatly improved. The new system was approved in 1942.

The role of topography was critical to efficient fire missions. But establishing the topography for divisional artillery required a minimum of six hours. The topographical officer would fix the coordinates of an arbitrary reference point (Divisional Artillery Check Point), which would be transmitted, to each battalion. If a map with reference grids was available, he gave each battalion the coordinates of two points, of which one would be situated inside the target zone. If the topographical exercise had not yet been carried out, an aerial reconnaissance photograph could be initially used for creating a firing table.

In order to train new personnel in just a few months, the firing manual was drastically simplified: for example it glossed over the calculations used for determining ammunition consumption related to a specific desired effect, as well as the detailed target acquisition procedures. In parallel with the objectives of centralization of control, everything in the manual, which was not strictly essential, was systematically eradicated – at least up until the start of the campaign in France – in order to simplify the task of the end user. In the same way, the information sent by the forward observer was easily and quickly transformed into firing instructions thanks to a simple method known as the "target grid", allowing cross-reference of the line between the observer and the target with the line between the gun position and the target.

Bombardment was carried out on a quick reaction basis – usually employed by the armored artillery – or to a prearranged plan. The latter could be initiated at the request of the infantry or on the initiative of the artillery commanding officer. Bombardments involving the concentrated fire of several battalions were the most effective, but were subject to certain pre-conditions: delivery of fire on the same point with the aid of topography or an adjustment fire, well known fire capacities of the battalions involved, sure and sound communications, and the FDC of each battalion well trained and employed.

The divisional artillery designated the units taking part and allocated them a part of the target. It was agreed that a battalion of 105s using indirect fire, with an interval of 50 yards between howitzers had an effective beaten zone of 200 yards x 200 yards, and one battalion of 155s or two of 105s had a beaten zone of 330 yards x 330 yards.

To ensure the safety of the infantry, it was absolutely forbidden to fire on a target designated by the general support battalion or a reinforcement battalion without having first obtained verification of its location from the divisional artillery or the direct support battalion concerned.

At the level of the corps, the fire maneuver was based on the same principals as those of the division, and a Corps Artillery Check Point was also to be established. But the FDC was often physically remote from the Artillery CP, normally set up too far behind the front line: the commanding officer of the corps artillery and his second-in-command would then split their task between the two locations. It could also happen, as was the case with XII Corps in September 1944, that two FDCs would be established because of the extended length of the front line.

AMMUNITION

For the purposes of planning and distribution, ammunition was grouped together into Class V, along with explosives and chemical agents. It was classified according to its use: service, practice or blank ammunition.

Artillery ammunition comprised a projectile, a propelling charge and the primer to set in motion the charge. It was termed:
— "fixed ammunition" when the shell case was crimped to the base of the projectile
— semi-fixed ammunition" when the base of the projectile was a free fit in the mouth of the shell case, permitting on site adjustment of the powder charge depending on the range required.

Each of these two types of round would then be loaded as one piece into the chamber.

For calibers of 155 mm and above, the ammunition was termed "separate-loading", the propellant charge being contained in one or more combustible bags loaded in the chamber behind the projectile.

During night firing, the excellent anti-flash properties of the propellant powders in use greatly hampered the enemy's ability to spot the battery, which was firing.

The most commonly employed projectile was the HE (High Explosive) shell filled with TNT, as shown by the allocation of this type (following combat experience) per caliber: 105 Howitzer, 75 to 80 percent; HE 155 Howitzer, 80 percent HE; 155 Gun, 90 percent HE. Above the caliber of 155 mm, virtually all shells fired were HE.

The HEAT variety (High Explosive, Anti Tank) filled with pentolite was used by weapons up to 155 mm caliber against tanks and bunkers. However, *"although the US Army in its publications made frequent reference to the HEAT shell, this was basically propaganda, since in the majority of cases it proved less effective in combat than the HE shell. Despite this, 5 percent of the ammunition supply per battery was HEAT, although it saw little use.[9]"*

Because the characteristics of the propellant charges could be subject to minor variations, when firing a barrage to be controlled by observers, it was recommended that the ammunition to be used should all be taken from the same batch. Any ammunition left over when fire ceased could later be used for harassing and interdiction fire by "wandering" pieces.

In reality, however, it was often difficult to ensure the delivery of ammunition all from the same batch to a particular

On February 17 1944 in front of Cassino, an ammunition handler of Battery A, 132d FA Battalion places the seven charges – white bags numbered from 1 to 7 – in a 105 mm shell case.

Shell HE M101 for the 155 mm Guns M1, M1917 and M1918.

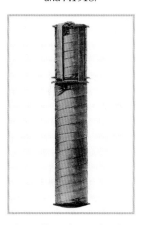

Propelling charge for the 155 mm Gun M1.

Propelling charge (White Bag) for the 8-inch howitzer

(National Archives)

9-Konrad F. Schreier, Tanks & Artillery.

The average weight of the main HE ammunition components in service was as follows:

	Shell as fired	Complete load semi-fixed round	Complete load + bag charge
75 mm Howitzer	14.6 lb	18,2 lb	-
105 mm Howitzer M2	33 lb	42 lb	-
105 mm How M3	33 lb	42 lb	-
4.5-inch Gun	55 lb	-	67 lb
155 mm Howitzer M1	99 lb	-	107 lb
155 mm Gun	96 lb	-	118 lb
8-inch Howitzer	200 lb	-	228 lb
8-inch Gun	240 lb	-	346 lb
240 mm Howitzer	360 lb	-	440 lb

battery, due to a lack of understanding of this requirement, or simply pressure of work by the personnel loading the ships or trains.

To pierce concrete, there was a special hardened steel fuze that reinforced the head of the normal HE shell. Using the "anti-concrete" fuze, at 1,000 yards it was possible for a 105 mm howitzer to pierce 5 feet thickness of concrete with ten closely placed rounds. The same effect required four rounds from the 155 mm howitzer and three from the gun of the same caliber. On the other hand, just one round from either the 8-inch or the 240 mm would go straight through.

Chemical projectiles came in several different categories according to their use:
— smoke shells filled with white phosphorus, zinc hexachloretane or oleum and sulphuric chlordrine

SHELL	COLOR	MARKING
High Explosive	Yellow or Olive drab	Black or Yellow
Armor Piercing (AP)	Yellow or Olive drab	Black or Yellow
AP or Semi-AP	Black	White
Smoke	Blue-gray Yellow bande	Smoke in Yellow
Incendiary	Blue-gray Purple band	Black
Gas		
transient effect	Blue-gray	Green band
persistent effect	Blue-gray	2 green bands
irritant effect	Blue-gray	1 red band

— incendiary shells filled with thermite or petroleum jelly (napalm)
— gas shells filled with phosgene, yperite or chloracetophenol.

The most common smoke shells were those giving off a red smoke, the two other colors – green and purple – being deemed less effective. Poison gas shells were stockpiled, but never used in action.

Shells were identified by their paint and markings:

Artillery ammunition supply was an unending task. The ammunition carried by each battalion varied: 190 rounds per piece for the towed 105 mm, 240 rounds for the S-P 105 mm, 110 rounds for the 155 mm.

But for the purpose of keeping units fully supplied with ammunition, the logistics experts worked out the following "units of fire[10]":

	Piece rounds	Battalion rounds	Division tons	Division rounds	Total tons
75 Pack How	80	960	10	2,880	30
105 How	175	2,100	50	6,300	150
105 S-P How	175	3,150	75	9,450	225
155 How	100	1,200	60	1,200	60
155 Gun	100	1,200	80	-	-
8-inch How	100	1,200	130	-	-

Below.
On May 12 1944, near Castelforte, a French artillery lieutenant acting as a forward observer officer reports with an SCR 610 the advance of tanks and "tirailleurs".

_____
10-Conventional unit of measurement used as the basis for calculating ammunition supply requirements, based on the experience of consumption during prolonged operations.
11-Almost forty, comprising four 76.2 mm and two 122 mm Russian guns, ten German 88s, eight 100 mm guns, six 105 mm gun-howitzers and six 150 mm howitzers, plus three pieces of French origin.

Compared with the well-publicized fuel shortage which affected the Americans in France during the summer of 1944, and which seriously hampered the drive to the Rhine, the continual shortage of ammunition was less-well known.

By the end of October 1944, with their consumption of ammunition continually increasing, the gunners had to put into service captured enemy artillery pieces, to maintain the required level of supporting firepower. In one week, 80 percent of the 12,000 shells fired by XX Corps came from this source.

And the following month, in order to offset the dramatic diminution in their own ammunition supply, they were obliged to continue to employ captured enemy pieces[11], with all the attendant problems of fire control this inevitably entailed.

LIAISON AND OBSERVATION

For the gunner, command communications are essential. However, his Field Manual 6-101 allowed a certain amount of latitude in this matter. The ideal situation would be that the commanding officer of the artillery battalion in direct support knew personally, and was on good enough terms with, the commanding officer of the infantry regiment, to work alongside the latter in his regimental CP. Some artillery commanders sent their executive officer instead, who might feel out of place and be relegated to the role of post box.

According to the manual, *"the command post of the infantry regiment and the CP of its direct support battalion should be in the same location as far as possible..."* however it was accepted that "limited means of communication and the requirement for efficient and rapid commands requires that the FDC be placed quite near the battery positions. The FDC should be situated inside the CP of the commanding officer of the battalion..." But finally *"experience has proved that the infantry regiment PC, after its second or third leap forward, is at a distance which requires the artillery move forward also, and in this way the two PCs will once more become completely integrated."*

To which certain gunners replied, that this was good in theory. They quoted the case of an aggressive infantry colonel whose CP was sited rarely more than 1,000 yards from his forward elements, while the artillery batteries would be positioned three times that distance behind the lines. Another case was that of a rapid advance, when the regiment was on the road and had no fixed CP, except at night. The same liaison problem would arise at battery level. Who should be with the liaison detachment alongside the infantry battalion: the battery commander or his second-in-command?

To cover the infantry, it was not enough to simply demand fire support (i.e. liaison). It was also necessary to ensure that the barrage fell in the correct place (i.e. observation).

Naturally, these two missions could not always be carried out from the same position. Liaison depended on the position of the CP or even where the commanding officer was situated. Observation required a presence on the ground. Each battalion had two liaison and observation teams, allowing them to both liaise with the infantry and at the same time establish an observation post. At the battery level, it was possible to carry out both functions but with more limited means.

The excellent qualities of the radio equipment and its wide range of applications transformed the establishment and the work of the observation and liaison detachment. The commanding officer was in continual contact with his subordinates, both when positioned and when on the move. Radio in particular eased the work of the battalion, most noticeably when moving forward – always the decisive moment in combat – during which phase all the elements in motion remained in contact with the commanding officers at all levels.

The battalion was allocated four radio wavebands. Each battery had its own frequency, which allowed it to fire on the orders of one of the officers (the battery commander, forward observer or liaison officer) without fear of being confused with the fire from neighboring batteries. All the combat radio sets in the 600 series had a pre-set common waveband, which could be, used when on the move or at rest, to ensure continuity of communication. The FDC for its part was provided with three radio sets, one of which linked it to the DA.

However, the limited number of wavebands available brought with it the need for rigorous discipline in utilization of the radio, and imposed the use of short messages. This in turn encouraged the large-scale use of the telephone in preference to the radio. Again, the telephone was the usual means by which the higher command levels passed orders to their subordinates.

The same principles of utilization applied to the corps artillery, which employed:

— a command network for the attached battalions using an SCR 284

— a permanent link to all the corps artillery on an SCR 608

— a fire control network on an SCR 193

— a post-to-post connection with the radio equipment of the tactical air forces.

At the same time that radio communications were profiting from technical advances, which provided them with powerful and simple to use equipment, the observation came to possess greatly

enhanced capabilities thanks to the introduction of specialized aircraft, constructed and reserved – at least in principle – for the exclusive use of field artillery.

Each battalion, group, divisional or corps artillery had the use of a section of two aircraft: normally the Piper L-4 Cub but occasionally a Stinson L-5 Sentinel. Easy to fly, taking off or landing on a short strip (100 yards), able to fly slowly enough for efficient observation, and fitted with an SCR 610 radio set, the Cub was the ideal aircraft for the artillerymen.

Situated at the center of an information network, the gunner at battalion level profited from a wide range of information coming from different sources: G-2 of higher echelons, photographic reconnaissance, prisoner of war interrogation, air observation post, forward or battery observer, observation battalion.

THE FIELD ARTILLERY OBSERVATION BATTALION

The observation battalion or FOB had three principal missions: spotting the position and determining the caliber of enemy batteries, adjusting the fire of friendly artillery, and exploiting intelligence.

The twenty-one battalions raised were generally attached to a brigade or t a corps.

Activated on 1 December 1934 at Fort Bragg, North Carolina, the 1st FA Observation Battalion received this designation in November 1940. At the beginning of August 1942, it sailed for England then reached North Africa on 6 December. It next landed in Sicily on 10 July 1943

On or around 20 August 1944, in the final stages of clearing the Plougastel Peninsular, officers of the 2d Infantry Division Artillery CP are connected by telephone to their forward observers facing Brest.

The 1st FA Observation Battalion followed the French from Italy to Alsace and ended the war with two citations. Its distinctive unit insignia evokes the three means of spotting enemy batteries: sound, flash and airburst shells.

A radio set with a range of 5 miles (8 km) used solely for voice communication, the SCR 609 had two pre-set wavebands in the range 27 to 38.9 megacycles, and could communicate with the SCR 608 and SCR 628 used by armored units.

Tunic of a Major of the 288th FA Observation Battalion attached to the First Army. (Le Poilu, Paris)

In Sicily on 1 August 1943, gunners observe the bombardment of Troina during the attack by the 1st ID. The officer on the right is relaying to the Fire Direction Center the information given to him by the one in the center using binoculars or the Telescope, Battery Commander, M65

and was at Salerno on 10 September, and acted in support of the corps of the Fifth Army up until the end of the war. During the offensive launched in May 1944, it was attached to the 13th Brigade, which supported the French Expeditionary Corps.

The 2d Battalion was formed at Fort Bragg in June 1940. It reached North Africa in September 1943 and landed in Italy on 19 November. In May 1944 (less its own Battery A but with the addition of Battery A from the 1st Battalion) it found itself on the left flank of the front with II Corps. Then on 11 August 1944, it landed in Southern France.

A third Battalion – the 15th, formed in May 1942 – passed via Northwestern Africa and arrived in Italy on 23 October 23 1943. In May 1944, it was with VI Corps in the Anzio beachhead, reinforced by Battery A from the 2d Bn.

Eight others were formed in the period June 1941 to June 1942 which, transiting by way of England, arrived in France between 7 June and 19 August 1944. Four battalions were planned to land in Normandy with the first waves: the 12th Bn on 7 June, the 17th Bn with V Corps on 8 June, the 8th Bn with XIX Corps on 26 June and the 13th Bn with VII Corps on 30 June. Eight Battalions numbered from 285th to 294th formed in 1943 and 1944 arrived directly on the Continent of Europe between September 1944 and February 1945.

In the Pacific, the 287th Bn activated in May 1943 fought in the Philippines in October 1944 then reached Okinawa in 1945. As for the 289th Bn formed in November 1943, it also fought in the Philippines from January 1945.

The battalion consisted of a headquarters and headquarters battery and two observation batteries.

The HHB was divided into five sections; topography (calculations and drawing up of plans), signals (radio and telephone), maintenance (day-to-day repairs) and services (supply, meals, vehicle repairs). In addition it took charge of administration and provided messengers and protection personnel.

Each observation unit was divided into four sections: sound location, flash location, signals and services.

In the sound location section, two teams of topographers carried out the work of the section and seven teams set up the central post and the advanced posts. The equipment consisted of six sensitive microphones operating on wavebands of 4 to 25 kilocycles per second placed in front of the central post and linked to it by wire. The microphones were placed equidistant from one another to triangulate the readings received. Installing the equipment took as long as the work of setting up the topography: between five and ten hours depending on the proximity of geodesic points of reference. The accuracy of the readings provided was of the order of 15 yards at ranges of less than 8,000 yards.

In the flash location section, electrical devices were replaced by observers equipped with precision binoculars, who marked the position of the muzzle flash when an enemy battery fired, recording the exact time with great precision. The section could also operate to spot and correct friendly fire. The time required for positioning varied between four and six hours, the topographical work taking most of that time.

The length of the observation base was a function of the lie of the land and the distance from the enemy battery positions, but it usually depended on the amount of time available for the setting up.

The battalion strength was 466, including 24 officers, and it was transported in some 90 vehicles[12].

MOBILITY

As with the other arms of service, which were, 100 percent motorized, the Field Artillery had at its disposal a large range of robust, well-designed motor vehicles. They were easy to handle and the hi-lo dual ratio gearbox fitted to virtually all units gave them great operational flexibility. In addition, a large proportion of the trucks were fitted with powered winches, highly appreciated for hard work and for getting out of difficult situations.

Four types were in widespread use:
— 4x4 1/4-ton light vehicle, the famous Jeep
— 4x4 3/4-ton Dodge light truck, and its command car, ambulance and 37 mm mount M6 derivatives
— 6x6 1/2-ton GMC truck, the famous "Deuce and a Half", used as tractor for the 105 mm and to transport personnel and equipment, plus its derivatives with a shelter for signals or a mobile workshop
— 6x6 4-ton Diamond truck, used as a tractor for 155 mm howitzers, with its wrecker version based on the same chassis.

For the armored division artillery, half-tracks replaced a proportion of the wheeled vehicles, and the battery forward observers rode in a Sherman tank still armed with its 75 mm gun.

The profusion of vehicles at their disposal enabled the demands from all units for additional mobile radio sets to be fulfilled. An SCR 193 set mounted on a Jeep was attached to each battalion, whether attached to a division or not, and each battalion and corps headquarters battery received two. The radios they carried were intended to work within the command network of the artillery of the corps and the army. Finally, each air observation post section received one Jeep fitted with either the SCR 510, 608 or 610, plus a Dodge 3/4-ton truck.

In a different role, the trucks played a vital role in resupplying the battalions. The transport capacity of a

[National Archives]

battalion of 105 mm howitzers was 2,829 rounds, divided between:

9 trucks with trailers (each 155 rounds) of the combat
echelon   i.e. 1,395 rounds
2 ammunition trucks with trailers (each 155 rounds)
per battery   i.e. 930 rounds
4 artillery tractors (each 42 rounds) per battery)
                   i.e. 504 rounds

In another example, the gasoline transportation capacity of the battalion was 3,168 US gallons – with one jerry can per Jeep, two per Dodge, three per GMC – making up four units of gasoline. The unit of gasoline was the amount of fuel used by the battalion to cover 62 miles (100 km). For a vehicle assumed to be in relatively new condition, and rolling along a route with moderate hills, a Jeep used 4 US gallons (15 liters), a Dodge 8 US Gallons (30 liters) and a GMC truck 10? US gallons (40 liters). The average range of the battalion using its on-vehicle gasoline reserve was thus 250 miles.

Taking into account their deadweight and bulk, heavy artillery pieces were obviously towed by more powerful vehicles. For the 155 mm gun and the 240 mm howitzer, initially the 6 t-on Mack or Corbitt 6x6 trucks were used. Then because of the problems encountered in emplacing or moving the pieces or simply towing them on-road, a whole series of high-speed tractors on caterpillar tracks was designed, to tow not only the heavy pieces, but also for the battalions of 155 mm howitzers.

Designed by Harvester in 1942, the M5 HST 13-ton used parts of the suspension from the light tank M5 and went into production in 1943. Although intended for the 105 mm howitzer, it was normally used for the 4.5-inch gun and the 155 mm howitzer. The ammunition was carried in a rear compartment which could hold 38 rounds of 4.5-inch or 24 rounds of 155 mm. The final batch of 589 tractors built were designated M5A1 with a larger cabin and a metal roof in place of the canvas tilt. By popular demand, from February 1944 a ring mount for a .50-cal machine gun (12.7 mm) was fitted in the crew compartment.

The M4 HST 18-ton, designed at the end of 1942 by Allis-Chalmers using certain parts of the medium tank M4, was intended to tow the 155 mm Gun or the 8-inch howit-

zer. Production started in 1943 with a model fitted with either a pannier for 30 rounds of 155 mm or one containing 20 rounds of 8-inch. The last 259 units constructed were the M4A1 having a better grip on soft ground. The M4C version could carry eight gunners and 48 rounds of 155 mm. Most battalions were equipped with the M4 HST, although a few retained their Mack tractors.

The M6 HST 38-ton was developed by Allis-Chalmers in February 1942. Closely resembling the M4, it could carry 10 gunners. But although approved in June 1943, it did not go into production until 1944. To make up for the late delivery of the M6, other expedients had to be used.

Thus the M33 was conceived, using the M31, a tank recovery vehicle derived from the Grant M3, devoid of turret and crane and which appeared in Italy in spring 1944 with the first battalion of 240 mm howitzers. But the shortage of available M31 TRV led to moves to transform M32B1 TRV (Sherman tanks stripped of their gun and fitted with a crane) into M34 prime mover conversion. Then the surplus production of M10 tank destroyer chassis was used to build the M35 PM used in Europe in 1944 by the 240 mm battalions. The M6 HST finally arrived in the spring of 1945, but in limited numbers.

The total production of this equipment was as follows:

	1943	1944	1945	Total
M4	1644	2911	1256	5811
M5	975	3503	1401	5879
M6	-	724	511	1235
M33	60	49	-	109
M34	-	24	-	24
M35	-	209	-	209
Total	2679	7420	3168	13267

All of these elements – from the ammunition to the gun tractor by way of the radio set and the light aircraft – allowed the Field Artillery gunners to rapidly lay down accurate fire with the appropriate weapon and ammunition, irrespective of the visibility or the terrain and in any weather.

These unparalleled performances were made possible by their first-class signals equipment, which optimized the efficiency of the fire control network and the work of the forward observers, and in particular the aerial observers.

A 155 mm Gun M1 battalion during the advance on Brest. It is a truck-drawn unit, in this case a 7-ton Mack NO truck. At that time, only two battalions in France were equipped with the new HSTs.

Mounted on towed artillery pieces, the Aiming Circle M1 was used to measure the angles of sight and azimuth. (Artillery Museum, Draguignan)

12-22 Jeeps, 39 Dodge 4 x 4 and 28 GMC.

(National Archives)

THE ARTILLERY OF THE INFANTRY DIVISIONS

*Shirt of a First Lieutenant
of the 109th FA Battalion with
the shoulder patch of the 28th ID.
(Le Poilu, Paris)*

WHEN measures were taken in the wake of the German victory in France, to flesh out the three component parts of the US Army, the artillery of the ten active Regular Army divisions was under-strength, and one sole corps had artillery units on its roster.

Mobilization of the National Guard, carried out between October 1940 and November 1941, allowed an increase in the number of available large formations. Thus one month later, thirty-three divisions, nine corps and four armies were in existence. But the Field Artillery, although having doubled its number of battalions in one year, still had only 80 on strength, the remainder of its units being still organized on the old regimental system.

Following field tests carried out in Texas in 1937 (and later in 1939) by the 2d Division1, and inspired by the example of the European armies, the ternary divisional structure was adopted on 1 January 1939. Then the success of German arms and the masterly way in which they deployed their combined arms combat formations accelerated the process of change in the US Army.

Although the manpower and equipment schedules[2] were not fully filled, the order was given to the first nine active

On 14 August 1943 some 20 miles from Messina, a battery of 105 mm Howitzers M2 supports the advance of the infantry of the 9th Division.

Regular Army divisions to pass over to the "Triangular" type on 1 October 1940, which involved the disappearance of the infantry and artillery brigades and of one infantry regiment in four. The divisions of the National Guard, called up for Federal service still on the old "Square" system, were restructured over the course of the first two months of 1942.

THE "TRIANGULAR DIVISION"

Then, all the large infantry units – except for the airborne divisions or those devolved from the Cavalry – were set up on a triangular basis, their number and type evolving each half-year, until in December 1944 there were on strength 66 infantry divisions, one mountain division and five airborne divisions.

For General McNair, the infantry division, supported by artillery, remained the basic war-winning element, to which the new forces – primarily the armored units and the Air Corps – would lend their assistance. He felt that a balance would need to be established between the different arms of service, the details of which would be determined by combat experience.

In 1941, when he sensed that the balance was not leaning far enough in favor of the new forces, he vigorously insisted that they be strengthened. Then the following year, when the United States was involved in the war and General McNair sensed the balance seemed to favor an unwarranted development, not only of the air forces and the antiaircraft arm, but also the armored and motorized divisions and the various specialized units, he appeared to some observers to be a conservative element, putting more emphasis on the infantryman and the field gun.

Within the reductions in manpower forecast for the ground forces in 1943, both the War Department and the Army Ground Forces agreed on the fact that shipping capacity was the determining factor. The War Department concentrated on cutting back on just the heavy units which they felt would cause the greatest transport problems, but the AGF preferred to reduce all those units, whether heavy or light, the shipping of which would add the least advantage to the Army's overseas combat potential. The AGF recommended that, from preference, the reductions should bear on the antiaircraft and the service units, as well as on the armored and motorized divisions, rather than on the infantry and airborne divisions.

In the final resort the WD applied the reductions to the heavy units and reduced the proposed numbers of armored and motorized divisions.

The infantry division was regarded as a large versatile unit conceived for classical operations in a theater of war, which allowed the use of motor vehicles. It possessed little by way of integral artillery and specialist units, its needs in these areas being supplied by the corps and the army.

Following the debate of ideas and the tests in the field carried out between the wars, its total strength went from 28,000 in 1918, to 24,000 in 1920, then to 13,600 in 1936, and finally to 12,545 according to the T/O 702 of June 1941 circulated just prior to the Japanese attack. This figure corresponded exactly with the objectives of General McNair, which were to deploy the maximum by way of force and mobility with the minimum expenditure in manpower, armament and tonnage to transport overseas. His formula nonetheless had certain disadvantages, notably a limited antitank and antiaircraft capability.

Organized along compound lines, the infantry division comprised essentially three infantry regiments – each of three battalions – which, when associated with three battalions of artillery each of three batteries, could form three regimental combat teams (RCT).

For the Artillery, the solution proposed in 1935 by a working party set up by the Army General Staff was not retained. It had been planned to attach to the divisional artillery a battalion of 105 mm howitzers for general support and three mixed battalions of 75s and 81 mm mortars for direct support. The 75 mm would be the French 75 Model 1897 on a new mount allowing it to be towed behind a truck or be elevated to fire against aircraft.

It was however clear from the field tests that the mortar was a short-range infantry weapon. And McNair felt that the long-range weapons grouped together could concentrate their firepower and yet retain flexibility. He also decided that the 105 – when available in sufficient numbers – should replace the old 75s in the direct support role, and that a battalion of 155s should form the centralized artillery battalion in place

A 105 HM2 howitzer is being hoisted onto a DUKW during an exercise. It was aboard these machines following the assault waves as closely as possible that the support batteries reached the beaches.

	Total	Infantry	Cavalry	Motorized	Light	Mountain	Airborne
31.12.41	29	29	-	-	-	-	-
30.06.42	37	33	-	4	-	-	-
31.12.42	58	52	-	4	-	-	2
30.06.43	69	63	2	-	-	-	4
31.12.43	73	64	2	-	3	-	4
30.06.44	73	66	1	-	1	-	5
31.12.44	72	66	-	-	-	1	5
31.03.45	71	66	-	-	-	-	5

of the 105s. From then until the end of the war, the divisional artillery would preserve virtually the same structure. However, by 1945 their manpower would nonetheless have reduced by more than 20 percent:

June 41	August 42	March 43	July 43	January 45
2,656	2,479	1,949	2,160	2,111

THE MANPOWER CRISIS

With the establishment of the T/O in March 1943, following the directives of the War Department and though General McNair was well suited to judging the requirements of his own branch, the AGF proposed that the manpower of the infantry regiments should be reduced by 11 percent and that of the divisional artillery by 22 percent.

The economies affecting the firing batteries would be less than a quarter of this planned reduction. The major part was to come from the fusion of the command batteries and the service units, which would free up some thirty truck drivers, mechanics, cooks and aid-men. But the greatest economy would come from suppressing the 52 men of the antitank section with their six 37 mm guns and the antiaircraft section, who were all charged with defending the battalion CP. The assignment of 16 rocket launcher (bazookas) and an increase in the number of .50-cal machine guns would provide immediate protection in an emergency, and its overall close-in protection would be left in the hands

Officer collar badge of the 109th Field Artillery Battalion, formed out of the 2d Battalion, 109th Regiment, Pennsylvania National Guard. (Le Poilu, Paris)

1-General McNair, who commanded the division artillery, played a key role in these field tests.
2-The Tables of Organization (T/O) replaced after 26 Aug 43 by the Tables of Organization and Equipment (T/O&E or simply TOE).

(National Archives)

Halted by the roadside somewhere in England, Battery C of the 32d FA Battalion of the 1st Infantry Division waits to embark on the ships that will transport them to Omaha Beach.

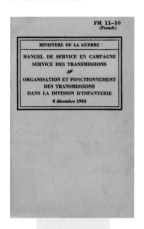

Field Manual 11-10 (French) published in 1943, on the organization and operation of signals in the infantry division. (Private Collection)

of surrounding infantry units. The basic armament would remain unchanged; twelve 155 mm howitzers and thirty-six 105 mm howitzers. But the total manpower, including the medical detachment, would fall from 2,555 to 2,002, the number of vehicles from 603 to 495, and the tonnage for sea transport from 12,000 to 9,000.

McNair also looked to reduce the number of auxiliary personnel in each division. As a result of his thinking, infantrymen and gunners would take on the simpler tasks common to all the arms of service. They would man their own radio and telephone posts, without the need for signals specialists, they would clear mines without recourse to the engineers, and would maintain or repair their own arms and their vehicles. The medical service was to be an exception, even though every soldier was to be given instruction in first-aid, and that each regiment or battalion had its own medical detachment.

He planned also that the regiments and battalions should deal directly with the service units under the control of the Army, and would arrive themselves in their own trucks to re-supply their units at depots set up nearby.

Prior to publication of these T/O, General Marshall asked for the reactions of the commanders in the various theaters of war. McNair therefore left for North Africa to investigate at first hand. Wounded soon after his arrival, he was therefore not in a position to explain the rationale behind his reductions, which was basically to save men to create new divisions. In any case General Dwight D. Eisenhower rejected the project out of hand, with the agreement of all his corps and division commanders.

At this point, in June 1943, the overall manpower situation was such that half a million men planned for the Army were taken away from it and 12 divisions were struck from

the mobilization program. At the same time, it was essential that McNair and Eisenhower find some common ground between them. The auxiliary units were mainly reorganized along the lines proposed by the former, while reorganization of the combat units followed the wishes of the latter. The cannon company of the infantry regiment was re-established, along with the service battery in each field artillery battalion. And because of operational experience in North Africa, the 57 mm guns replaced the 37 mm anti-tank guns.

The T/O were finally published on 15 July 1943. The divisions still in the United States were reorganized on 1 September 1943 and those overseas in the following months. The 1,250 men freed up from each larger unit constituted a total of 82,500 who went to form six divisions in addition to the 60 existing ones.

Anticipating the landings in France, on 12 January 1944 the War Department announced that the European theater would require an additional 50,000 infantrymen and gunners by the summer. The replacement training centers being unable to supply this number of men, the AGF therefore had to find them from somewhere, without halting or delaying the formation of new units. One solution appeared to be to reduce the basic training period to just thirteen weeks, instead of the required minimum of seventeen.

Next it was decided that the reinforcements should be taken from every unit of the AGF not assigned for service overseas in the near future, and being men who had at least nine months training. However, since it proved impossible to guarantee that all the reinforcements – of whom 80 percent were to be infantrymen – would have received this level of training, and also this measure would seriously

A 105 mm Howitzer M2 in action during the battle for Brest.

(National Archives)

impede the later transfer overseas of the depleted units, the only solution was to go back to basics. Thus it was that between 15 January 1944 and 31 March 1945 the reinforcements were found by principally disbanding antiaircraft units.[2]

THE DIVISONAL ARTILLERY HEADQUARTERS

The divisional artillery consisted of a headquarters and headquarters battery, three light artillery battalions and a medium artillery battalion. Each of these four battalions had a headquarters battery, a service battery and three firing batteries.

A brigadier general, controlling the organic and attached field artillery units, and serving as artillery adviser to the divisional commander, is in command. To assist him he had an executive officer with the rank of colonel. Each

"Somewhere in Germany, 1945", a round is loaded into a 105 mm Howitzer M2, while the artificer screws the fuze on a shell and the ammunition numbers prepare the following rounds.

(National Archives)

Distinctive unit of the 3d Division Artillery, inherited from the 3d FA Brigade disbanded in October 1939. (Le Poilu,

officer also had an assistant who would be a lieutenant or second lieutenant.

The headquarters consisted of four officers:
— a lieutenant colonel, head of operations (S-3)
— a major in charge of intelligence (S-2)
— a lieutenant attached to the S-2, charged with reconnaissance and observation
— a captain in charge of personnel and logistics (S-1 and S-4).

A captain, who was also the communication officer, with two Jeeps and one trailer, commanded the headquarters battery[3].

The personnel and equipment of the operations platoon were divided into four sections:
— operations

— instruments and survey
— meteorology
— air observation with two Piper L-4 Cub light aircraft.

The communication platoon was divided into:
— a wire section (telephones)
— a HQ & message center (radio).

The maintenance section then the AM&S (Ammunition, Maintenance & Supply) team completed the organization.

Close-in defense was provided by three .50-cal (12.7 mm) heavy machine guns[4], of which one was assigned to protect the Piper Cub landing strip, and by six rocket launchers M1.

The radio equipment comprised two 284 sets, two

105 MM HOWITZER M2A1, CARRIAGE M2A2

Having noted that 105 mm light howitzers had been used by German, Austrian and Italian artilleries during the Great War, the Westervelt Board recommended the adoption of a weapon of this caliber, which, because of budgetary restrictions, would initially replace only the 155 Schneider in one of the divisional battalions.

The first prototype inspired by the German howitzer was built in 1920, then three improved models appeared in 1927, featuring a split trail and pivoting axle, mounted on wheels with pneumatic tires. However, no production models followed, and the US Army continued to deploy the Great War artillery pieces, which had been modernized[1], principally by fitting them with pneumatic tires. At the time the infantry division possessed two regiments of 75s and one of 155s.

The initial tests of the 105 mm Howitzer M2 carried out at Fort Sill

in 1932 were basically satisfactory. Improvements were incorporated in the recoil brake – to permit firing at a high angle without the need to dig a deep hole under the breech – and to make the mounting more suitable for towing by motor vehicles.

A first batch of 48 howitzers was ordered in 1939 and the final version of the mounting was adopted in March 1940. The M2A1 model with all the latest improvements was ordered into mass production in April 1941.

In the course of the war two further improvements were incorporated.

The brakes operated from the tow vehicle were removed to bring the weight below the maximum permissible limit of 5,000

1-75 mm Gun M1917A1 derived from the British 18-Pounder, 75 mm Gun M1897A2 (High Speed), 75 mm Gun M2 and 155 mm Howitzer Model 1918A3 based on French models.

(National Archives)

608 sets and two 610 sets. The telephone equipment setup was one telephone switchboard BD-71 with six lines, two BD-72s with 12 lines and 19 handsets EE-8.

In practice, however, the theoretical personnel strength varied constantly between 1941 and 1945:

THE LIGHT DIRECT SUPPORT BATTALION

Each towed 105 mm howitzer battalion[5] was commanded by a lieutenant colonel, assisted by a staff of seven officers.

The headquarters battery counted six officers, including the captain commanding the battery and two pilots, a warrant officer plus 111 enlisted men. Apart from the light aircraft section, it basically had an operations section composed of fire control and observation teams,

plus two liaison detachments. Four other sections looking after signals, antiaircraft and antitank defense, personnel and maintenance.

Its equipment comprised:
— eleven Jeeps, of which five had a trailer and three were fitted with wire reel unit
— six command cars and eight Dodge 4x4s with winches, of which three were fitted with reel unit
— three 2 1/2-ton trucks, two of which with trailers.

The personnel of the service battery – four officers, one warrant officer and 69 enlisted men – were charged with administration, vehicle maintenance and supply. The latter function was assured by three transport groups, each one having four 2 1/2-ton trucks with three 1-ton trailers and one ammunition trailer. In addi-

3- T/O et T/E 6-10-1.
4-Three .50-cal Browning M2 HB: one on a tripod M3 and the other two on AA mountings M3.
5-T/O and T/E 6-25.
6-Provided by three .50-cal Browning machine gun (one on an AA mounting and two on tripods) plus four bazookas.

pounds (2,300 kg) and a revised gun shield was fitted at the insistence of General McNair. By a large margin, the M2A1 was the US Field Artillery piece constructed in the greatest numbers, its production running from April 1941 up to June 1945:

1941	1942	1943	1944	1945	Total
597	3 325	2 684	1 200	730	8 536

170 battalions were equipped with the howitzer – three battalions in each infantry division and four per cavalry division – divided between 141 in Italy, France and Germany, and 61 in the Pacific.

Under the terms of the Lend-Lease Act[2], 16 105 mm howitzers were delivered to Great Britain, 637 to China, 68 to France[3] and 60 to the countries of Latin America, principally Brazil.

The howitzer comprised an elevating barrel assembly of 105 mm caliber, on a pivoting mounting with split trails and an oscillating axle with two pneumatic tires. The barrel assembly comprised a short barrel with semi-automatic breech block, with constant long recoil controlled by an oil and pneumatic recoil brake. The howitzer came with either mounts models M1 or M2 or, in the case of the self-propelled version, the S-P Gun Motor Carriage M7.

The howitzer was normally towed by a "Deuce and a Half" GMC truck with winch.

The crew comprised chief of piece section, gun-layer and seven gunners: elevation layer, loader, fuze setter, assistant fuze setter and three artificers.

The weapon was extremely effective against personnel in the open or behind light cover; it was capable of destroying machine gun and anti-tank gun emplacements as well as barricades and light obstacles. Used in low angle fire, it was effective against medium tanks out to 550 yards.

Specifications:
Weight in traveling order	4,980 lb
Length overall	19.5 ft
Width	7,25 ft
Width in firing position	11.8 ft
Weight of mounting	2,490 lb
Weight of barrel and breech	1,064 lb
Weight of one wheel	269 lb
Tire size	3 x 24 inch
Tire pressure	448 psi
Traverse	46°
One turn of the traversing hand wheel	20 mils
Elevation	0° to +64°
One turn of the elevating hand wheel	10 mils
Maximum rate of fire	10 rounds per minute
Rapid rate of fire	4 rounds per minute
Sustained rate of fire	2 rounds per minute
Max rounds in 5 minutes	20
Max rounds per hour	100
Barrel life	approx 7,500 rounds
Maximum deviation in 12,000 yards	43 yards
Time for positioning	2-3 minutes

Muzzle velocity and maximum range per charge:

Charge	Muzzle velocity in feet/sec	Maximum range in yards	Range at 65° elev. in yards
1	640	3,830	2,735
2	700	4,375	3,280
3	768	5,030	3,830
4	860	6,125	4,700
5	1,004	8,200	6,000
6	1,214	9,950	7,200
7	1,552	12,200	8,860

THE BATTERY OF FOUR HOWITZERS POSSESSED THE FOLLOWING FIRE CAPABILITIES		
Neutralizing linear target	100 yards of front line	36 rounds in 2 minutes
Neutralizing in-depth target	10,000 square yards	80 rounds in 5 minutes
Standing barrage	200 yards of front line	80 rounds in 5 minutes
Smoke barrier	200 yards of front line	60-80 rounds in 5 minutes

The security range for infantry is 300 yards.

2-Passed on 11 Mar 41, the Act, which was also known as the "Defense of the United States Act", authorized the President to sell, hire or lend basically military equipment to the government of any country of which he deemed the defense to be vital to the interests of the United States.
3-According to Steven J. Zaloga in US Field Artillery of World War II. In fact, the French armed forces possessed 180 HM2s divided between four divisional artilleries and one group of the general reserve.

A 105 mm Howitzer M2 of the 1st Infantry Division in action at Kasserine Pass in February 1943.

7-T/O and T/E 6-35.

nition trailer. Close-in defense relied on four .50-cal machine guns – two on high-angle mountings and two on tripods – and eight rocket launchers (bazookas).

For signal duties, the battery used four SCR 610 sets, two BD-71 telephone switchboards and eight EE-8 field telephones.

On the road, by day the length of the battalion column was 9,600 yards and the time taken to pass a given point was 17 minutes.

At night the column closed up to a length of 4,800 yards.

	1.6.41	1.8.42	1.3.43	15.7.43	24.1.45
HHB, Div Arty	119	116	111	114	114
Band	29	28	-	- -	
attd Medical	83	76	53	57	57
Lt Arty Bn (x 3)	584	576	460	509	497
Hqs Btry	142	165	181	132	126
Svc Btry	82	78	-	77	74
Firing Btry (x 3)	120	111	93	100	99
Med Arty Bn	785	607	458	519	506
Hqs Btry	142	158	164	115	112
Svc Btry	95	89	-	77	76
Firing Btry (x 3)	134	120	98	109	106
Antitank Btry	146	-	- -	-	
Total	2768	2583	2002	2217	2168

tion the battery possessed two Jeeps plus one trailer, and three Dodge 4x4s.

As noted earlier, the headquarters battery and the service battery were combined by order of the T/O of March 1942 into one headquarters & headquarters and service battery with less personnel and vehicles in the combined unit.

Finally, three firing batteries each had five officers plus 94 enlisted men. They were divided up into three specialist teams – command and fire control, reconnaissance and ammunition supply – and four gun crews with one 2 1/2-ton tow truck per howitzer. Their other vehicles were four Jeeps, one dedicated to the observers having a trailer, four Dodge 4x4s and three 2 1/2-ton trucks, two with 1-ton trailers and one with ammu-

THE MEDIUM GENERAL SUPPORT BATTALION

The battalion of towed 155 mm howitzers[7] was also commanded by a lieutenant colonel, assisted by a staff of seven officers. Its organization was similar to that of the 105 mm battalion, but its personnel strength differed slightly.

The personnel of the headquarters battery was composed of four officers, one of whom was the captain commanding the battery and two others were pilots, plus one warrant officer, and 109 enlisted men.

As well as two light aircraft, it possessed eight Jeeps, of which three were fitted with telephone cable reels and three 1/4-ton trailers, three command cars, five Dodge 4x4s with winch, of which three carried a telephone cable reel, and two 2 1/4-ton trucks with 1-ton trailers.

The service battery was composed of four officers, one warrant officer and 71 enlisted men. It possessed two Jeeps with one trailer, three Dodge 4x4s, 13 2?-ton trucks with three 1-ton trailers and nine ammunition trailers, plus one wrecker.

Each firing battery had four officers and 102 enlisted men. It possessed three Jeeps with trailers, four Dodge 4x4s, eight trucks with three 1-ton trailers and one ammunition trailer.

Initially they were armed with the Howitzer M1918, derived from the French Model 1917 Schneider, manufactured in the United States with a slightly modified breech and a redesigned gun shield.

Because of its bulk and weight, in the early 1920s the Westervelt Board recommended that the 155 mm should be passed on to the corps when the new 105 mm howitzers arrived in the divisions.

A 155 mm Howitzer M1918A3 during exercises circa 1938.

On 1 October 1944, while the 91st Division attacks towards Bologna, a 6 Ton truck towing a 155 mm Howitzer M1 penetrates a smoke screen covering Route 65.

(National Archives)

However, given the delays in obtaining the latter howitzer, in 1929 the 155s were reissued to the Divisions. Then in 1933 General MacArthur decided to motorize the Field Artillery and to modernize two-thirds of the artillery pieces. So a new carriage M1918A1 was adopted, of which the most noticeable feature was the provision of wheels with pneumatic tires. Between 1936 and 1940, 600 howitzers of this type out of a total of 3,000 in service were modified in this way to become the M1918A2 which was known as the "High-Speed" model. Further modifications resulted in the final version, the M1918A3. Then in view of more delays, this time in delivery of the 155 mm M1, 35 additional howitzers were modified in 1940, another 1,162 in 1941 and a final batch of 218 in 1942, making a grand total of 2,014.

On the road, the length of the battalion column was 10,800 yards (9,900 m) by day and 5,400 yards (4,950 m) by night. And the time taken to pass was 20 minutes.

MOVES TOWARD REDEPLOYEMENT

Beginning in January 1945, the Army Ground Forces planned to set up new organization and equipment schedules – renamed Redeployment T/O&E – to take account of operational experience. The start date of February 20 was set for reorganizing the infantry divisions, and a study of their support echelons would follow. The AGF intended that the R Tables would form the basis of the post-war setup.

To achieve this end, the War Department set two preconditions:

— elimination of dual assignments that required personnel to perform secondary duties to the detriment of their primary function (for example, cook's helpers, switchboard operator or vehicle drivers)

— inclusion in the tables of certain items ordinarily provided to theaters in "special lists of equipment" that experience had shown were essential to normal operations, along with the personnel to operate them. The AGF therefore put forward their plans for change in three categories:

— Plan #1 – changes generally required by the troops in the various combat theaters, not involving the reorganization of the divisions, but eliminating the double functions and incorporating the changes required by the War Department (especially regarding signals)

— Plan #2 – as for Plan 1, plus minor modifications such as the inclusion of self-propelled howitzers in the cannon company of the infantry regiment

— Plan #3 – as for Plans 1 and 2, plus certain overall changes which were deemed necessary, such as the attachment of a tank battalion.

A group of officers from the AGF were sent to Fort Benning, Georgia, in order to record the experiences of Major General Fred H. Walker, commanding officer of the School of Infantry since 24 July 1944, and who had previously formed then led into combat the 36th Infantry Division of the Texas National Guard. The results of the study were

(National Archives)

On 26 January 1945, in the Apennines, a 155 mm Howitzer M1 of the 34th Division takes part in a harassing fire.

finally put before the War Department on 8 March, including the following notes on how the proposed changes

BATTALION			
	Officers	NCOs	Increase
T/O & E - 1.3.45	143	1948	-
Plans #1 and #2	163	2386	+ 438
Plan #3	176	2416	+ 43
	+ 33	+ 448	+ 481
DIVISION			
	Officers	NCOs	Increase
T/O & E - 1.3.45	763	13 274	-
Plan #1	775	15 219	+ 1967
Plan #2	812	16 669	+ 1487
Plan #3	867	17 418	+ 804
	+ 104	+ 4 138	+ 4 258
	Officers	NCOs	Increase
T/O & E - 1.6.45	787	15 081	+ 1831
	+ 24	+ 1 807	

would impact on the total manpower of each infantry division: The increases concerned primarily the signals (telephone operators, switchboard staff, radio operators), the fire control echelons, the ammunition handlers and the forward observer teams. Also, since combat reports indicated that two pilots were not enough to ensure necessary rotations and relieves, two extra officers were planned for each of the division HQ and the four battalions. One other significant change was the disappearance of the forward observer team from the battalion and the creation of a similar team within each battery.

In addition, the commission led by Major General Albert W. Waldron proposed that a battalion of 4.2-inch mortars should be included, but this was rejected.

THE END OF THE WAR

On 5 April 1945 the War Department signified its approval. However, because of the probable serious effects of the changeover phase, none of the three plans was put into immediate effect. Certain improvements were in fact permitted, such as the attachment of additional personnel to (see on left)
— the headquarters battery of the divisional artillery, for counter-mortar duties (4 officers and 47 enlisted men)
— each 105 mm battalion, for counter-mortar and communications duties, as well as to increase the number of howitzers per battery from four to six
— the 155 mm battalion, for communications duties (17 enlisted men).
Finally, after a series of slight adjustments, a new schedule was published on 1 June 1945. The totals of the various proposals for the infantry division stacked up as follows:

	1.3.45	8.3.45	1.6.45
Crew	14 037	18 285	15 838
Vehicles	2 113	3 630	2 564

On 29 May 1945, the War Department issued orders to the European and Mediterranean theaters to either put into effect the reorganization program according to the new T/Os before leaving Europe, or to send to the United States those personnel involved in the reorganizations.

In July 1945 gunners of the 334th FA Battalion of the 87th Division prepare their 105 mm Howitzers M2 for transport back to the United States, and eventual redeployment to the Pacific Theater.

(Le Poilu, Paris)

Distinctive unit insignia of the 125th Field Artillery Battalion, 34th Infantry Division formed in January 1942 out of the 2d Battalion, 125th Regiment of the Minnesota National Guard.

155 mm HOWITZER M1, CARRIAGE M1A1

(National Archives)

The 155 mm Howitzer M1 entered service late, due to lack of funds, but also because of delays caused by discussions on the best caliber – 155 mm or 4.7-inch – plus technical problems primarily concerning its weight. Even when the decision to go ahead was taken on 15 May

1941, production did not start until the end of 1942, because of lack of industrial capacity. The efforts of the factories during 1943 allowed the divisions taking part in Operation Overlord to be fully equipped in time for the invasion of Europe.

After the 105 mm and 75 mm, the 155 mm M1 was the howitzer most in use. It equipped 163 battalions: 49 divisional battalions and 78 in the General Reserve in Europe, 22 in Italy and 14 in the Pacific. In addition, under the terms of the Lend-Lease Act, 236 howitzers were delivered to Great Britain, 36 to China, 12 to France 11 and 18 to Brazil.

The nine man crew were initially transported in GMC trucks. But beginning in July 1943 two types of vehicle were used: truck-drawn by the Diamond 4-ton and tractor-

Production ran between October 1942 and June 1945, as follows					
1941	1942	1943	1944	1945	Total
-	19	1469	1949	598	4 035

drawn by the Caterpillar High Speed Tractor M5. In the case of the latter, the battery would be issued with six M5s and two Diamond trucks.

The battery of four howitzers possessed the following fire capabilities:

Neutralizing linear target — 100 yards of front line — 24 rounds in 3 minutes

Neutralizing in-depth target — 10,000 square yards — 40 rounds in 5 minutes

Standing barrage vs personnel — 200 yards of front line — 1 battery in 5 minutes

Standing barrage vs armor — 100 yards of front line — 1 battery in 5 minutes

Smoke barrier — 200 yards of front line — 60-80 rounds in 5 minutes

Illumination — 150 yards diameter — Duration one minute — 2 rounds per howitzer in 2 minutes

Weight in traveling order	13,000 lb
Overall length	20.3 ft
Height	6.6 ft
Traverse	870 mils
Maximum elevation	1120 mils
Average rate of fire	2 rounds per minute
Rapid rate of fire	3 rounds per minute
Sustained rate of fire	3 rounds per minute
Time for positioning	5 minutes

MUZZLE VELOCITY AND MAXIMUM RANGE PER CHARGE

Charge	Muzzle velocity in feet/sec	Maximum range in yards	Range at 65° elevation in yards
1	680	4,287	3,200
2	770	5,360	3,675
3	886	6,780	4,855
4	1017	8,596	6,500
5	1,214	10,772	8,200
6	1,510	13,430	10,400
7	1,854	16,350	12,800

Shell flight time at maximum range	60 seconds
Time for positioning	5 minutes

1-Steven J. Zaloga, op. cit. During the Liberation Campaign the French Army possessed 60 Howitzers M1 in two divisional battalions and three battalions of the general reserve.

Then in July the plans were modified once again. Those divisions in the Pacific theater were to undergo progressive reorganization as and when circumstances

	1.3.45	8.3.45	1.6.45
HHB, Div Arty	114	150	130
Lt Arty Bn (x3)	497	609	538
Hqs Btry	126	159	158
Svc Btry	74	90	74
Firing Btry (x3)	99	120	102
Med Arty Bn	506	615	529
Hqs Btry	112	142	126
Svc Btry	76	95	76
Firing Btry (x3)	106	126	109
Total	**1 117**	**1 374**	**1 197**

permitted, and subject to the availability of the necessary men and materials. The first divisions redeployed via the United States would be dispatched with an additional 1,800 men each, to be reorganized on their arrival in the Southwestern Pacific Area. And in order to speed their deployment to the Pacific, the five divisions still in the United States would be reorganized with men supplied by the European and Mediterranean theaters.

In the plan dated March 15 1945, it was planned to reduce the number of infantry divisions from 65 to 50. However, the end of hostilities intervened before the planned measures could be put into effect. In fact only two divisions – the 86th and the 97th – would reach the United States in June before being redeployed to the Philippines and Japan, and they would see out the war without having been committed.

Canon and panoramic telescope for the 105 HM2. (Artillery Museum, Draguignan)

Below: M5 tracked tractors and 155 HM1 howitzers moving along a German road in 1945.

[National Archives]

Then in July, the series of repatriations began:

	Europe	Italy	Pacific
July 1945	7	-	-
August	1	1	-
September	6	1	-
October	2	-	2
November	5	2	1
December	5	-	2
January 1946	5	-	1
February	-	-	2
March	3	-	1
Total	34	4	9

Technical Manual 9-325 published on 10 August 1944 by the War Department, dealing with the 105 mm Howitzers M2 and M2A1 plus their different carriages. (Private Collection)

During this period, seven divisions were inactivated in Japan, Korea or the Philippines, and two were inactivated in Germany, one in Austria, one in Italy and four in the Far East.

Four years later, when the Korean War broke out, seven infantry divisions were once more activated: five from the Regular Army and two from the California and South-Western States' National Guards. All of these units were organized on the lines of the scheme drawn up in 1945.

155 MM HOWITZER M1918, CARRIAGE M1918A3

The short-barreled 155 mm howitzer was widely used in the Pacific and in Tunisia. But after the appearance of the M1, it was progressively replaced, except for those theaters having a lower priority, such as Italy or the Pacific, where it continued in service up until 1943[10].

SPECIFICATIONS

- Weight in traveling order — 9,590 lb
- Overall length — 22.3 ft
- Height — 6.56 ft
- Traverse — 52 mils
- Maximum elevation — 750 mils
- Average rate of fire — 2 rounds per minute
- Rapid rate of fire — 3 rounds per minute
- Sustained rate of fire — 1 round per minute
- Maximum range — 12,250 yards
- Time for positioning — 4 minutes

———
1-The French Field Artillery had 60 howitzers equipping two divisional battalions and three battalions of the general reserve.

(National Archives)

THE ARTILLERY OF THE SPECIALIZED DIVISIONS

D ESPITE the opposition of the Army Ground Forces, among the 71 large units with a predominance of infantry formed between 1941 and 1944, there appeared at times a number of divisions which approximated to the structure of the triangular division, but whose manpower and equipment differed according to their specific mission.

Actually, General Leslie J. McNair disapproved of the formation of units organized for certain missions or special surroundings, such as airborne, mountain or jungle units. He preferred to provide specialist training to a classic infantry division, and to attach to it a number of experts in the specific role and environment.

However, while the cavalry divisions were losing their mounts and the airborne divisions were undergoing rapid expansion, between 1941 and 1943 the AGF Headquarters had to bow to the pressure of demands from the War Department for a series of tests with specialized "light" or motorized divisions.

As a result, as the following table shows, the numbers of large formations fluctuated over the years depending on the plans and requirements of the theaters of operations (see page 35):

THE EXPERIMENTAL MOTORIZED DIVISION

Inspired by the Germans who deployed truck-borne motorized divisions to cover the vulnerable flanks of their Panzer Divisions against counter-attacks, in November 1940 the War Department announced that the US Army intended to equip itself with this type of large formation.

This motorized division should therefore possess sufficient motor vehicles to allow it to transport all of its elements at one time, in order to cooperate closely with the armored units. It should comprise some 16,000 men and a greater number of support and supply elements than in standard large formations, since it was supposed to act in an independent fashion, at least for short periods. Its mission – primarily defensive – was thus to cover the flanks and rear of the armored divisions, so that they could concentrate on their primary mission which was to forge ahead as rapidly as possible.

The 4th Division, activated on 1 June 1940 at Fort Ben-

The 1941 edition of the Gunnery Manual used at Fort Sill. (Private Collection)

A 75 mm Pack Howitzer M8 of one of the parachute battalions created towards the end of 1942, during training on the airstrip near Fort Bragg in North Carolina.

	Motorized	Light	Mountain/Jungle	Cavalry	Airborne
23 May 42 OPD[1] estimates	23	-	4	1	7
30 Sep 42 AGF recommendations	13	4	-	2	6
25 Oct 42 G-3[2] recommendations	10	8	-	2	6
29 Oct 42 AGF proposals	5	-	-	2	6
24 Nov 42 WD decision	10	-	-	2	6
15 Mar 43 WD authorizations	1	-	-	2	6
14 Apr 43 AGF recommendations	1	8	-	2	6
1 Jul 43 WD decision	-	1	-	2	5
15 Jan 44 WD decision	-	3	-	2	5
1 Jul 44 WD decision	-	1	-	1	5
1 Jan 45 WD decision	-	-	1	1	5

ning, Georgia, was chosen for the tests. It was redesignated "(motorized)" on 1 August, and then became the 4th Motorized Division in July 1941. In November of that year it participated in the major maneuvers in the Carolinas as part of IX Corps. At the end of its training period, the 4th took on the aspect of a powerful, and extremely mobile, light armored division – more offensive in capability than defensive – with 14,000 men and 2,600 vehicles.

In view of the results obtained by the Ist Armored Corps

during the November maneuvers, Major General Jacob L. Devers, in command of the Armored Forces since August, asked for a motorized division attached to each of the four armored corps in existence or planned. However, the AGF judged as premature the formation of a fixed "type" corps, with a formation of motorized infantry attached to it.

The Carolinas maneuvers also demonstrated that it was advisable to combine one motorized division with every two armored divisions. Therefore on 9 April 1942, three new larger units were officially transformed into motorized divisions: the 6th in Missouri, the 7th in California and the 8th in South Carolina. The following month, the Operations Division (OPD) in Washington, DC estimated that 23 of the 140 divisions to be mobilized by the end of 1943 should be motorized. To this the AGF retorted that this number was excessive and did not correspond in any way to the current transport situation. Nevertheless, on 15 September 1942 the 90th Infantry Divisions in Texas was transformed in its turn into a motorized unit. The 9th Infan-

try Division at Fort Bragg, North Carolina, was slated for conversion in April, but after having undergone amphibious training on the Atlantic coast, it was designated to participate in Operation Torch in North Africa. One part of its elements was put ashore in Morocco on 8 November 1942, with a battery of 75 mm pack howitzers attached to each of its six battalions involved in the landings[3]. Then with the rest of the division following in December, it was regrouped near Oran where its 75s were progres-

sively replaced by 105 mm Howitzers M2. Finally on February 17 1943, following the arrival of its last two artillery battalions[4], the whole force set off on a forced march to the Kasserine Pass on the Tunisian Front.

A PROJECT CUT SHORT

In reality only the 4th Division – initially designated in August for service overseas – received the total strength of appropriate men and equipment. All the changes required of a motorized unit were obviously reflected in its Artillery elements, which had to adapt as and where necessary to the new organizational structure and tactical concepts.

Its manpower strength and amount of equipment[5] allowed for a total of 16,889 men – of which 3,427 were infantry and 2,479 gunners – plus 2,879 vehicles[6], practically all devoted to the combat role, including 18 S-P 75s, six towed 105s and 12 towed 155s.

Influenced by the Panzer Divisions, in which the Germans were increasing the number of infantrymen, Gene-

A 75 mm Pack Howitzer M1 during training.

*Below left.
A 75 mm Pack Howitzer in action in Anzio Beachhead.*

In service with the Philippine Scouts in the 1930s, this 75 mm Gun M1897A4 was the improved version of the French gun manufactured in the USA with pneumatic tires.

1-Operations Division of the War Department General Staff.
2-G-3 Division of the War Department General Staff.
3-84th FA Battalion with the 47th Infantry at Safii and the 60th FA Battalion with the 60th Infantry at Port-Lyautey.
4-26th (105) and 34th (155) FA Bns with the 39th Infantry.
5-T/O 77 of 1 Aug 42.
6-I.e. 730 more than the existing divisional strength and 867 more than the total planned

Reactivated in June 1940, the 4th Infantry Division served as the experimental motorized division, then moved to England in January 1944 and landed on Utah Beach on 6 June 1944. (Private Collection)

ral Divers became convinced that his formations were deficient in infantry. In August 1942, while the 7th Division participated in maneuvers with the II Armored Corps in the Desert Training Center in California, he requested that the motorized divisions should become "mechanized" or "armorized", in other words that their Infantry element should be organized in the same manner as their armored division counterparts.

Although he passed on this request to the War Department, McNair recommended on the one hand the assembly of 25 infantry battalions in half-tracks, who could reinforce the armored divisions as the need arose, and on the other hand the reduction of the current program to create five additional large Motorized formations. His proposals were accepted in February 1943 and a decision was taken to reconvert all the existing motorized divisions into standard larger units. On 1 January 1943 the 7th Division reverted to "infantry" once more, then the 90th, the 8th and the 6th followed in May.

However, the Operations Division of Army General Staff wished to keep the 4th as a motorized division in order to maintain a core of personnel trained in a method of deployment on which it had not yet made up its mind. Then the commander of the European theater, whose opinion had been sought, responded in June that no motorized division featured in his invasion plans for the following year. So on 4 August the 4th was reconverted to a normal infantry division in its turn. It was also decided that all infantry divisions should undergo training in movement by motor column, being reinforced at least in theory by six truck companies per division.

In the course of the operations in Europe, several infantry divisions were temporarily motorized, in whole or in part, and usually during an advance. However, this was not accomplished by using the Quartermaster Corps trucks, which were dedicated continuously to logistical re-supply, but thanks to vehicles borrowed from temporarily immobilized antiaircraft units.

The light Divisions

From 1942 onwards, it became clear that the Army would have to be prepared to fight in various climatic conditions – such as Norway, Libya or Malaysia – and to make use of various means of delivery, amphibious or airborne. The problem was to decide how many specialized units should be created.

For his part, General McNair, working on the basic principles of flexibility and economy of effort, did not agree with dedicating significant resources to meet specific problems. He felt that basic training provided in this way would be to the detriment of general military competence, and he felt it was futile to give men detailed instruction in skiing, gliders or landing craft which would be used only for a strictly limited period. His solution was to provide specialized training as and when required for a specific operation, to men who had already received their basic military training. In addition, such specialized training could be given in situ during the enforced waiting period while the elements of the special operation were being pieced together.

During the summer of 1942, with the looming prospect of an offensive in the Southwest Pacific Theater, the Operations Division began to work on training troops to fight in mountainous terrain and in the jungle. For such work, the classic division possessed too many heavy weapons and vehicles to be able to move with ease in mountainous terrain, in dense forests or where there were no

A 75 mm Pack Howitzer M1 of the artillery attached to the 32d Division during training on 20 May 1943 at Camp Gable in Queensland, Australia.

Shoulder patch of the 71st Infantry Division. Formed specifically in July 1943 for jungle warfare, it took on a more classic role in May 1944 and finally left for France in January 1945. (Private

February 24 1944 on the Burma border, Brigadier General Frank D. Merill, commanding Galahad Force, watches as a column of pack mules carrying 75 mm ammunition passes by. (Department of the Army)

permanent roads. At the beginning of August, a study was initiated into the formation of a large unit numbering 10,000 men, who would be lightly equipped for jungle operations. Even before the program was finalized, at the end of August it was planned to form three mountain and jungle divisions. In October, while a reduction in land forces was being proposed in order to reduce the tonnage to be transported overseas, the experience of those units sent to England during the summer of 1942, and of those preparing for Operation Torch in November or already engaged in the offensives in the Solomons or New Guinea showed that it would be inadvisable to simply reduce in size an existing standard infantry division. As a result, the OPD proposed the formation of divisions.

Conceived as large multipurpose units, capable of being deployed when the local situation imposed a limit on the amount of equipment which could be transported, they were particularly suited to amphibious, airborne, mountainous or jungle operations. For these missions they used respectively landing craft, gliders, pack mules or native porters. The OPD, inspired by certain Japanese units, also examined the possibility that light divisions could operate without vehicles or even animal transport. Their overriding advantage was that they would occupy less shipping space.

General MacArthur, commanding the Southwestern Pacific Theater, was agreeable to tests on a divisional basis, but he preferred that the units that would compose the light division should be trained in his command area and under his supervision. In that, he was in agreement with General McNair who preferred to create a training center for jungle warfare in the Canal Zone or even in the future theater of operations rather than in Florida or Louisiana.

He was however opposed to the formation of jungle and mountain divisions for the reason that they would rely on porters and mules to carry the major part of their supplies. He wished to employ a minimum of animal transport, and he opposed the formation of divisions that relied on them, for the reason that they would then be restricted to specific combat theaters. For this reason he wanted to restrict this aspect to the experimental stage, limited to the drawing up of suitable operational procedures and the specialized training of several infantry regiments and support elements. By using such personnel as a core to train others it would thus be possible to rapidly form specialized divisions as and when the need for them was proven.

JEEPS, PACKS, MULES AND HANDCARTS

In January 1943, when the War Department instructed the AGF to draw up appropriate tables of organization for light divisions, General McNair felt more able to accept them than the previous proposals, as they no longer called for an extreme degree of specialization, with all its attendant disadvantages. Although the light division was undeniably weaker than a standard type of large unit, it was to possess an equivalent firepower, would be easier to transport by sea, and be less demanding to re-supply and maintain.

The project submitted on 2 March envisaged a division of some 9,000 men, organized on triangular lines but with two elements reduced in size. For transport, it possessed only the utility handcart and, for operations in snow, the sledge. It could be employed in the various specialized theaters previously mentioned on condition that it received appropriate methods of re-supply: pack mules, light vehicles or porters. The divisional artillery, which comprised only three battalions of 75 mm pack howitzers, was to be the exception, with a permanent establishment of pack mules or Jeeps.

As the planned reorganizations had to balance resources with requirements, the AGF proposed in April the use

HE and antitank M66 shell for the 75 mm Pack Howitzers M1, M2 and M3.

A horse-drawn 75 mm Gun Model 1897 as used by the divisional artillery brigades during the 1920s.

of the strength freed up by the suppression of nine standard divisions from the 1943 program to create eight light divisions in the program for 1944. For its part, in May the G-3 put forward the figure of ten light divisions formed by the conversion of six infantry and four airborne divisions.

General Eisenhower, to whom the project was submitted, thought that this type of large formation held little interest for him, given the type of terrain in his combat theater. On the other hand, Colonel F. D. Merill, who acted as the representative in Washington[7] for Lieutenant General Joseph W. Stilwell, commander of the land forces in the China-Burma-India Theater, declared that the proposed light division closely resembled the Chinese divisions which had been reorganized in the theater of operations, and that it could operate with success in the jungle and mountain terrain as well as certain regions of China. As for General MacArthur in the SWPA (Southwest Pacific Area), the theater for which the light division had been basically conceived, he was of the opinion that it lacked sufficient firepower and logistical support to be employed on the Pacific islands.

Proceeding with caution, the WD authorized in June 1943 the formation of just one light division for tests purposes, to be converted from an existing large unit. On the other hand, the AGF, being of the opinion that it was time the units of the Mountain Training Center[8] were reformed along divisional lines, recommended the formation of a second division using pack animals. Then, returning to the idea of a large jungle combat formation, it proposed a third light division to be trained in the same means of transport.

On 21 June, the WD finally gave its consent to the formation of firstly two then three specialized Light Divisions to be converted from existing units. The 71st (Pack, Jungle) was activated on 15 July at Fort Carson, Colorado, with two infantry regiments brought back from the Panama Canal Zone – where they had already trained in jungle operations - and a third regiment specially formed in situ, plus three battalions of 75s formed three months later. The 10th (Pack, Alpine) was also formed on 15 July at Camp Hale, Colorado, with several units drawn from the Mountain Training Center.

Finally, the 80th Light Division (Truck) was formed by conversion of the 80th Division on 1 August 1943, also at Fort Carson.

7-And future commander in Burma of Marauders, who have passed their legacy on to present day American Special Forces.
8-Mountain Training Center activated at Fort Carson, Colorado in 1942.

Shoulder patch of the 89th Infantry Division. Reorganized as a light division one year after its formation in July 1942, it lost its specialized status in July 1944 and reached France in January 1945. (Private Collection)

	25.1.44		28.7.43
	Division	Divisional Artillery	FA Battalion
Officers	470	110	28
Warrant-officers	16	5	1
Enlisted	8 189	1 399	333
Total	8 675	1 514	362
Handcarts	555	91	-
Jeeps	267	116	34
Light aircraft	8	8	2
Rocket launchers	74	56	16
.50-cal Browning	79[9]	60	8
75 mm Pack Howitzers	48	48	12

THE 71ST AND 89TH LIGHT DIVISIONS

The new divisions were organized around three infantry regiments and three battalions of 75 mm pack howitzers, which were subject to continual development following field trails. In the 89th for example, the battalion of three howitzer batteries was enlarged to four.

However, while the 71st and 89th were engaged in a series of exercises intended to test their abilities and equipment, the officers of the Southwest Pacific theater continued their opposition to the formation of additional light divisions which they felt would be badly suited to amphibious operations. They thought that the 75 mm howitzer should be replaced with the 105 mm and that the Jeep should give way to a vehicle capable of carrying a heavier load, irrespective of the cost, notably of shipping.

Speaking out against their attitude, which he felt to be over-conservative and costly, McNair intervened in November 1943 on the side of the War Department. He noted that the SWPA needed one ton of supplies per man per month to maintain their 272,000 men, of whom one half was combatant. During the same period, five standard divisions would require 173,000 tons, and eight light divisions only 54,000 tons.

On the other hand, as the WD had allowed a wide degree of latitude to each theater commander to utilize the shipping at their disposal, it was clear that the SWPA would not voluntarily accept the attachment of a light division, unless under duress.

As a result, at the conclusion of the current tests with light divisions, it was thought essential to consider not only how they should be organized but also to ascertain whether the commanders of the various combat theaters still preferred the standard division. While awaiting the outcome of these deliberations, it was felt imprudent to proceed with the formation of additional light divisions.

The training phase finished with maneuvers – the 71st versus the 89th – in California from February to May 1944. Carried out in a mountainous region, practically devoid of roads and in high temperatures, they were the subjects of an analysis by III Corps that had run the war games. The report was severely critical:

— an additional quota of pack mules and vehicles had been necessary in order to continue the exercise

— the handcarts had been shown to be inappropriate and extremely fatiguing

— engineers had to be called in to open up tracks for the mules and jeeps

— the infantry regiments had been forced to allocate between a third and one half of their combatants to improve the tracks and carry supplies, leaving the equivalent of only six battalions available for combat.

In conclusion, Major General John Millikin considered that a light division could not survive any length of time unsupported. He advised that the classic formation should be adhered to, with the specialized units and their pack animals (field artillery and transport) being retained in the General Reserve, from whence they could be issued as and

A 75 mm pack howitzer of the 10th Mountain Division in action in January 1945 in the Apennines to the northwest of Pistoia.

when the need arose, to standard infantry divisions engaged in mountain warfare.

In any case, the War Department decided to end the matter. At the close of the war games[10], the 89th was sent to New Jersey where it reformed with its original configuration and designation on 15 June. It then took ship for Liverpool, and landed on Utah Beach on 3 August before going into action near Le Mans.

For its part, the 71st returned to Fort Benning where it became an "Infantry" Division on May 26, after exchanging its 75 mm pack howitzers against 105s and receiving in addition a newly formed battalion of 155s. In January 1945, despite its having been formed for jungle combat, it was designated as an urgent reinforcement division for the European Theater where the German counter-offensive in the Ardennes was in full swing. Taking ship in New York, it arrived in Le Havre on 16 February and fought in Lorraine after undergoing a month of retraining near Yvetot.

THE 10TH MOUNTAIN DIVISION

The end result was that the first two light divisions had been unable to overcome the resistance of the theater commanders to their use as replacements for standard divisions, because a large part of the infantrymen would be employed in maintaining the lines of communication and in the transportation of supplies. Nevertheless, despite the fact that the one-month delay imposed on the 71st Division to be ready for deployment had confirmed the limits and the disadvantages of too great a degree of specialization, and the misgivings of the AGF, the light mountain division was retained.

The 10th Light Division (Pack, Alpine) was activated in

Shoulder patch of the 10th Mountain Division. A light division specialized in mountain warfare from the time of its formation in July 1943, it reached Italy in January 1945. (Private Collection)

9-19 were attached to the quartermaster truck company which had 149 Jeeps.
10-In his order of battle, Shelby L. Stanton suggested that, contrary to the official texts, the 80th had indeed participated in the maneuvers in California, but only between December 1943 and March 1944.
11-T/O 6-155, 156 and 157 dated 4 May 43.
12-1125th Armored FA Bn activated on 25 Sep 44 at Naples out of the 454th Antiaircraft Automatic Weapons Bn.

Loading of a 75 mm Pack Howitzer M3 into a Waco glider during an exercise in North Africa.

Telescope BC M65, Battery Commander's scope used for observation and for angular measurement. (Militaria Magazine)

wardens, mountain rescuers and even Austrian refugees from the Anschluss. But the tests were disappointing. In order to avoid splitting up such highly qualified personnel, in November 1944 it was decided to convert it into a "special mountain division" of 14,000 men, with over 4,000 vehicles and some 6,000 pack animals.

The 10th Mountain Division was then offered to various theater commanders, who refused it because of its specialized equipment. Finally Lieutenant General Mark W. Clark, commanding officer of the Fifth Army, inherited it: having had to employ standard units in mountain regions for many months, he apparently had no regrets about his latest acquisition.

Its elements returned to Virginia to take ship at Hampton Roads for Italy, where its first echelon arrived two days after Christmas 1945. After a brief period of training, and with the addition of a 105 mm battalion[12], it went into the line on 8 January 1945 to the north of Pistoia.

BY PARACHUTES AND GLIDERS

While the majority of experimental divisions disappeared quickly because the rationale behind their formation was recognized neither by the High Command nor by their eventual users, the number of divisions intended for landing by air continually increased throughout the war.

Although the Americans were the first to consider landing a mass of troops by parachute behind enemy lines as early as 1918, it was not until May 1939 that the Chief of Infantry proposed the formation of an airborne infantry unit, which was hotly disputed by the Air Corps and the Corps of Engineers. The airmen wanted the airborne troops to be named the "Air Grenadiers" and be placed under their control, while the engineers thought they should be attached to their Corps, since their mission was to carry out sabotage behind enemy lines.

After several months of discussion, on 1 January 1940 the War Department charged the Chief of Infantry with studying the practical aspects of airborne infantry and their specific requirements by way of air transportation. Next the creation of an experimental platoon was authorized and on July 1, the Parachute Test Platoon was formed at Fort Benning, seat of the School of Infantry, with volunteers from the regiment attached to the school. Then the Air Corps re-entered the arena on 5 August with an attempt to control the future parachute units. But General McNair, who had just taken over as head of the GHQ, insisted that the ground forces retain them since the aircraft was only a means of transport, and in fact they would be committed in a ground role.

July 1943 at the Mountain Training Center, the basic function of which was to test specialized equipment and supervise the specific training of the units attached to it. Its elements were initially three infantry regiments activated at

	Hqs & Sce Battery	Firing Battery	Total
Offiiers	11	4	23
Warrant-officers	2	-	2
Enlisted	93	117	444
Total	106	121	469
Aircraft	2	-	2
Pack 75 How	-	4	12
Jeeps	1	-	1
1/4 ton trailers	1	-	1
He-Mules	16	3	25
SheMulet	86	55	251
SCR-2841	-	1	
SCR-6098	3	17	
EE-8	5	3	14

Camp Hale in Colorado: the first in May and the other two in July. Then in February 1944 one of the latter units was replaced by the 87th Infantry Regiment, which the previous summer had participated in the operations in the Aleutian Islands in the Northern Pacific. Its artillery was formed at Fort Carson: two battalions of 75 mm pack howitzers in January and a third in July.

These battalions were initially organized on the lines of the current tables[11]. With a lieutenant colonel in command, they comprised a headquarters and service battery, and three firing batteries, plus a medical detachment of around twenty men, of whom a quarter were given veterinary training. Their internal structure was similar to that of a 105 mm battalion, but with less men and of course the presence of pack animals.

The 10th remained in Colorado in order to undergo intensive training in mountain terrain and in snow. It counted in its ranks skiers and famous alpine climbers, park

	Division	Div Arty	FA Bn
Officers	673	100	31
Warrant-officers	43	6	1
Enlisted	12745	1682	333
Total	14101	1788	365
Light Aiircraft	8	8	2
75 mm How	36	36	12
.50-cal Browning	85	30	9
Rocket launchers	223	-	-
Jeeps	167	19	4
Dodge 4x4	43	3	1
Dodge 6x6	25	-	-
GMC	170	1	-
Animals	5961	1266	413
of which pack animals	4546	1057	347

On 16 September 1940, a first battalion of parachutists was activated, followed by a second on 1 July 1941. At the same time experiments began into using gliders to transport men and equipment. However, the initial results were often unsatisfactory because of excessive losses during landing accidents and the perennial shortage of tow planes. When enough aircraft had been assembled, a battalion of airborne infantry and a mixed artillery battalion took part in the Carolinas maneuvers.

In August, the Army General Staff G-3 advised the Air Corps that it was planning the creation of an airborne combat team comprising an infantry battalion, an antitank company, an artillery battery and a medical detachment. Tests were carried out into dropping the 75 mm Pack Howitzer by parachute. Then the Chief of Field Artillery was charged with creating a battery by February 1942, the Chief of Ordnance supplying the howitzers once the gunners had received parachute training from the Infantry.

On 11 December 1941, learning from the lessons of the exercises the previous month, Brigadier General Harry L. Twaddle, head of operations at the General Staff, recommended that the four existing battalions should be grouped together. On 24 February, at the suggestion of McNair, the War Department decided to expand each of the existing battalions to form four regiments, while plans were put in hand for the formation of howitzer batteries.

However, when the GHQ became the AGF, the two battalions stationed in Panama[13] did not automatically come under its control. Also, on 23 March, one of McNair's first actions as head of the AGF was to create the Airborne Command at Fort Benning[14], under Colonel – later Brigadier General – William C. Lee, who a year earlier had been the first to bring up the idea of forming a special airborne division.

Finally, on 24 September the 456th Parachute Field Artillery Battalion was formed out of the elements of the Parachute Test Battery. It would form the basis of all the new battalions that followed.

THE AIRBORNE DIVISIONS

The employment of an airborne division[15] was considered for the first time in March 1942, when the plans for a landing in Western Europe were drawn up. In fact, two larger units would ultimately be created on 16 August 1942.

Activated in March, the 82d Division – with the attachment of a number of parachute troops – would become the 82d Airborne before returning to Fort Bragg on 3 October. Once they had exchanged their 105 mm howitzers for 75 mm pack howitzers, two of its battalions became glider units. They were joined by two parachute battalions also equipped with the 75 mm pack howitzer, officially activated the day after the creation of the division on 24 September.

The 101st Airborne Division was directly activated on 15 August at the same location. At first it comprised two glider battalions, both previously activated in March as part of the 82d, one of which was initially trained on the towed 105 mm. Having exchanged these for the 75 mm pack howitzer, both battalions left the 82d and joined the 101st. And a parachute battalion was formed at Fort Bragg to complete its artillery component.

These were divisions of less than 9,000 men in total, but having all the elements of a classic larger formation plus an antiaircraft battalion. They initially comprised a parachute infantry regiment with three battalions, two glider infantry regiments of three battalions apiece, and three

artillery battalions headed up by a headquarters battery. For movements on the ground, each one possessed a total of 408 vehicles with 239 trailers.

The parachute battalion was composed of a headquarters and service battery, three batteries each with four 75 mm pack howitzers, and an antiaircraft and antitank battery. The two glider battalions each had, initially, two, then three batteries of four 75 mm pack howitzers.

In practice, the organization of each of the divisions evolved as their particular requirements changed. For example, on 12 February 1943, on the eve of its departure for North Africa the 82d adopted a T/O of its own which took

T/O 15.10.42	Division	Artillery
Officers	464	79
Warrant officers	29	8
Enlisted	7710	1337
Total	8203[16]	1424
Parachutes	2323	431
75 mm pack howitzers	36	36
.50-cal Browning	105	58
Rocket launchers	182	177
Handcarts	179	20
Jeeps	283	102
Dodge 4x4	20	1
GMC	82	10

13—501st Parachute et 550th Airborne Infantry.

14 - On 4/09/1942 it moved to Fort Bragg in North Carolina, while the Parachute School was opened at Fort Benning on 5/06/1942, and soon took on the function of a staff depot while the center itself undertook parachute training.

15 - The designation of "Airborne" was initially reserved for parachute units or for airlanding units. Ultimately it came to refer to all units transported by plane.

16-Plus 302 men and 16 jeeps for the medical detachment and the chaplains.

16 June 1943 at Oujda prior to the Sicilian invasion, a 75 mm pack howitzer belonging to Battery A, 320th Glider Battalion of the 82d Airborne is stowed inside a Waco glider.

(National Archives)

account of the reinforcement elements thought necessary.

Thereafter, and until the summer of 1943, the Airborne Command set up three other airborne larger units. Their fortunes would differ significantly.

The 11th Airborne was activated on 25 February 1943 at Camp Mackall, an annex of Fort Bragg in North Carolina. It was made up from a parachute regiment formed in January and two glider infantry regiments activated the same day, as was the glider artillery battalion and one of the two parachute artillery battalions, the second having been formed the month before.

Having participated in the combined airborne exercises, which took place during December in the Carolinas, the division took ship at San Francisco and arrived in New Guinea on 25 May. On account of the combat situation in the Southwest Pacific theater and the Philippines, it fought primarily on the ground, only a few of its regiments carrying out airborne or amphibious operations.

The 17th Airborne was formed less than two months later, on 15 April 1943, again at Camp Mackall. After taking part in a series of maneuvers, it took ship at Boston for England, then arrived in Mourmelon on Christmas Day 1944. It had the same composition as the 11th, plus

one parachute battalion added as reinforcements.

Last of all, the 13th Airborne was activated on 13 August 1943 at Fort Bragg, with the same organization as the last two others. It left New York on 26 January 1945 and, after three weeks of training near Fecamp, it set up base at Auxerre. For a lack of transport aircraft, it did not participate in the Rhine crossing.

AIRBORNE ARTILLERY IN COMBAT

For their part, the 82d and 101st were heavily reinforced for combat operations by the addition of separate units up to regimental size. Initially numbering 8,505 men, in June 1944 their theoretical establishment was 8,596, swollen to 9,115 with their usual reinforcements, to fall to 8,556 one year later.

The airborne larger units in fact evolved in the opposite direction to that which General McNair wished to follow. In November 1943, Major General Matthew B. Ridgway, commanding the 82d, in effect requested that they be made up to the size of a standard infantry division. General Devers, at that time in charge of the European Theater, gave his approval, but McNair opposed the move because he preferred to convert them into light divisions.

17-In the Pacific, the 11th Airborne Division retained its original T/O. 18-In fact only two parachute battalions of the 82d were equipped with 105s, thanks to the arrival of the Curtiss C-46 Commando, used for the Rhine crossing. All the other battalions retained their 75s.

75 MM PACK HOWITZER M1A1, CARRIAGES M1, M3 & M8

Inset. Breast patch of the 460th Parachute FA Battalion formed in April 1943 and attached to the 1st Airborne Task Force for the invasion of Southern France. (Private Collection)

This was the model produced in the largest numbers and used successfully in the Pacific, Burma and Italy.

The 75 mm Pack Howitzer M3 was developed in parallel for mounted artillery. After several modifications it was adopted in 1937 and was ultimately capable of being horse-drawn or towed by motor vehicle. But as the batteries were dismounted in 1943 without having gone into combat, for lack of a better piece it was employed by the Armored Cavalry in either its towed version of mounted on a Half-Track.

Load #1 – Barrel	244 lb
Load #2 – Cradle and upper sleigh	240 lb
Load #3 – Lower sleigh and brake mechanism	216 lb
Load #4 – Trail (forward part)	236 lb
Load #5 – Trail (rear part)	236 lb
Load #6 – Wheels and breech mechanism	228 lb

The carriage of the M1A1was a single articulated boxes trail. Traverse was effected by slewing the barrel assembly to one side or another on the axle, and coil spring equilibrators compensated for the weight of the barrel. Dismantling of the latter into several parts was quick and simple, the breech block and barrel mating through interrupted threads requiring just one eighth of a turn to unlock and lock. The whole howitzer could be split into six loads:

The M3A1 carriage was the mounting specially designed for towing at high speed (25 mph, 40 km/h) with either a six-horse harness or a 1? Ton caterpillar tractor. It was of the split trail type, opening out 46°5, with spring equilibrators and alloy disk wheels with pneumatic tires, mounted on anti-friction bearings and fitted with standard automobile brakes. It could be fitted with a gun shield.

At the close of the 1930s, the Artillery was also looking for a light howitzer to accompany airborne infantry. The choice fell on the M1, fitted to a chassis with pneumatic tire wheels replacing the wooden wheels to allow

Following the recommendations of the Westervelt Board for a new howitzer capable of transport by pack animal, the 75 mm Pack Howitzer M1 was adopted in 1927, after many trials and changes. It was planned for deployment in mountainous regions or on ground impassable by towed artillery. It could be broken down into several pack loads, or be towed by a single mule.

However, for lack of funds, less than a hundred were available in 1941. The delay was turned to advantage however, by improving the original weapon, and in particular the breech block, which then became the M1A1.

	Prcht 75 Pack How Bn T/O 6-215 24.2.44	Glider 75 Pack How Bn T/O 6-225 1.8.44
Officers	39	44
Warrant officers	2	3
Enlisted	542	345
Total	583	392
Light aircraft	2	2
75 Howitzers	12	12
37 mm AT Guns	4	-
.50-cal Browning	23	9
Rocket launchers	70	50
Handcarts	12	6
Scooters	12	7
Jeeps	18	43
Dodge 4x4	1	3
GMC Trucks	15	4

However, the European Theater came to have increasing influence and the death of McNair put an end to further objections.

A new T/O-71T (T for Test) was hastily drawn up based on the lessons drawn from the combat operations in Europe.

Completed on 16 December, it was immediately sent urgently to the divisions, who because of the combat situation were unable to put them into practice until 1 March 1945[17], just three weeks prior to the Rhine crossing. The new division bore a striking similarity to that suggested by Ridgway, with two parachute infantry regiments and one single of glider infantry, one 105 mm howitzer battalion[18] and enlarged support and service units. They now had an establishment of 12,979 men, or 13,906 with reinforcements.

T/O		June 1943	June 1944	June 1945
Div Arty	6-200	1474	1476	1394
	6-200T			1977[19]

The artillery as well as the infantry underwent similar variations, reflected in the tables of organization:

Their component units – notably the regiments following the reorganization of March 1945 – underwent frequent moves.

In the parachute battalion:
— the 460th Bn left the 17th Airborne for Italy in

Converted to Airborne five months after its formation in March 1942, the 82d Division participated in most of the large air assaults: Sicily, Salerno, Normandy and Nijmegen. (Private Collection)

towing by a Jeep. The howitzer therefore became the 75 mm Pack Howitzer M8 (Airborne) or, in accordance with US Army terminology, the 75 mm Pack Howitzer M1A1 on Carriage (Airborne) M8, with the same characteristics as the M1 except for the weight of 1,327 pounds (602 kg) and a normal towing speed of just 10 mph (16 km/h).

Intended to be loaded into a transport aircraft or a glider, on the ground it was towed by a Jeep. Then in 1943 a system of seven parachutes known as "paracrates" was designed for it to be airdropped, for the first time during the invasion of Southern France in August 1944.

It had a crew of seven; chief, aid, aimer, loader, firer, artificer and two ammunition gunners. Two howitzers were normally grouped together under the orders of a section chief that had the use of a radio, plus a messenger on a lightweight motorbike.

Load #1 – Wheels		Sling
Load #2 – Barrel		Container
Load #3 – Breech mechanism, gun sight		Container
Load #4 – Lower sleigh, gonio-compass		Sling
Load #5 – Trail (rear part), axle		Sling
Load #6 – Cradle, upper sleigh		Sling
Load #7 – Trail (front part)		Sling

To be dropped by parachute[1], it was broken down into seven loads:

Weight in traveling order		Horse-drawn M3	3,335 lb
		Towed M3	2,094 lb
Weight positioned	M1	1,270 lb M1A1	1,327 lb
	M3	2,094 lb	
Overall length	M1	12.14 ft M3	12.92 ft
Width	M1A1	4 ft M3	5.7 ft
Height	M1A1	3 ft M3	3.9 ft
Tire size	550x20	M3	
Tire pressure	30 Psi		
Horizontal traverse	5° M1 & M1A1	M3	45°
Per turn of the traversing handwheel		20 mils	
Elevation	90 mils M1; 220 mils M1A1 & M3		
Per turn of the elevating handwheel		24 mils	
Rapid rate of fire		6 rounds/mn	
Sustained rate of fire		3 rounds/mn	
Barrel life		12,000 rounds approx	
Max muzzle velocity		1,250 ft/sec	
Min muzzle velocity	700 ft/sec	Mxm range 9,460 yards	
Time for positioning		1 to 2 mn assembled; 3 mn disassembled	

Almost 5,000 75 mm Pack Howitzers – the majority being M8 models – were produced between September 1940 and December 1944:

1940	1941	1942	1943	1944	1945	Total
36	188	1208	2592	915	-	4939

Out of these, 826 were delivered to Great Britain under the Lend-Lease Act, 637 to China, 68 to France[2] and 60 to the countries of Latin America. In US Army in 1944-45, they equipped only 36 battalions, including 22 divisional units in Europe and three in the Pacific.

1-Type G1, Weight: 28.6 lb; diameter of the canopy: 24 feet; carrying capacity: 300 lb at 150 mph.
2-Of which some 40 were supplied to the 4th Moroccan Mountain Division and the rest were retained for the post-war airborne division.

Shoulder patch of the 1st Cavalry Division, a larger unit of the Regular Army maintaining more or less all of the structures and designations of the mounted troops. The First Cav became a "special" division in Australia in December 1943, comparable in fact to the standard IDs. (Private Collection)

19-56 officers, seven warrant officers and 2,838 enlisted men.
20-The two others were the 92d and 93d Infantry Divisions, which went into action respectively in Italy and the Pacific.
21-Brigade of cavalry: 4,278, divisional artillery: 1,920.
22-159th FA Bn (Cld) (105 mm How Trac-D) disbanded on 15 Jan 44 in Montana. The 77th Bn (Cld) (75 mm Horse-Drawn) was officially disbanded on 26 Feb 44, two days before leaving from Hampton Roads and the 79th on 10 Mar 44 in Oran.

June 1944 in order to take part in the Dragoon operation, and was attached to the 13th Airborne in February 1945
— the 466th Bn replaced the 460th in the 17th Airborne on 1 March 1944
— the 463d Bn took part in Dragoon, and was then attached to the 101st Airborne on 9 December, to be absorbed into the 101st on 1 March 1945
— the 464th Bn arrived in France on 24 February 1945 to become part of the 17th Airborne, but did not join it until 1 June.
As for the glider battalions:
— the 472d was formed in July 1945 in the Philippines for the 11th Airborne with elements of a battalion that had exchanged its towed 105s for 75 mm Pack Howitzers
— the 674th of the 11th Airborne became a parachute unit in the Philippines on 20 July 1945.
When the re-deployment from the European theater was being planned by the War Department, the five airborne divisions were to be reduced to three. At that point the AGF suggested that, man-for-man, two infantry divisions should be replaced by two airborne, for the simple reason that, not only was their combat potential at least the equal of a standard division, but their presence alone represented a threat which obliged the enemy to retain behind his front lines reserves which were sorely needed further forward.

THE ARTILLERY
OF THE CAVALRY DIVISIONS

In early 1945, virtually all of the large specialized or experimental units formed in 1942 had either disappeared, or had lost most of their specialized functions. The motorized and light divisions had been in existence for only a brief period, and only the pack mules, which furnished a large part of its transport requirements, now differentiated the sole mountain division. The airborne division alone survived and even multiplied. But in its manpower establishment and its organization it had come to resemble more and more a classic infantry division, differing only by its special manner of going into action.

As for the two cavalry divisions extant when the war started, one would adapt to the new forms of warfare and the other would disappear along with its horses.

The 1st Cavalry Division stationed at Fort Bliss, Texas, took part in the major war games of 1941. With close on 11,000 men and more than 9,000 animals, it comprised two brigades each of two cavalry regiments, two battalions of horse-drawn 75 mm howitzers and one battalion of towed 105 mm howitzers. As for the 2d Cavalry Division, activated in April 1941 at Fort Riley, Kansas, it was incomplete and only had two battalions of horse-drawn 75s. In May 1942 the decision was taken to keep them mounted, mechanization being reserved for regiments and squadrons not attached to a division and to the Cavalry units which were an integral part of infantry and armored divisions.

Finally the 2d was partially inactivated in July 1942, for lack of manpower and to complete the formation of the 9th Armored Division. The 1st was completely reorganized, with the following theoretical strength and equipment (at right):

While retaining its brigades and "square" structure, it now comprised two battalions of 75s and one battalion

	Division	Artillery
Officers	528	91
Warrant officers	48	7
Enlisted	11085	1900
Total	11661	1998
Scout cars	26	3
75 mm Howitzers	24	24
105 mm Howitzers	12	12
.50-cal Browning	280	64
Jeeps	445	54
Dodge 3/4 ton	233	85
GMC truck	329	95
Saddle horses	5407	504
Draught and pack horses	1342	480
Mules	299	-

A 75 mm howitzers
of a field artillery regiment
(horse) being positioned
for a fire exercise.

of 105s and had swollen to a total of 12,112 officers and men.

Then on 25 February 1943 the 2d was reactivated at Fort Clark in Texas, with the designation of Cavalry Division (Horse) (Colored), with two cavalry brigades and two battalions of 75s and one of 105s, all brand new. Of mixed color from its inception, it now became one of the three colored divisions[20], in other words soldiers of Afro-American origin commanded by white officers.

The transport of its animals, however, took up a great deal of shipping space, and at first no plan was drawn up for the overseas deployment of the two Divisions. Nonetheless, as the Southwest Pacific Theater could be deemed suitable, at the end of June 1943 the 1st was sent to Australia, with a total establishment of 13,258 officers and men – or 12,724[21]as its nominal strength

without its reinforcing units – which was virtually the size of a standard infantry division. On 4 December it took on the title of 1st Cavalry Division, Special, and moved to New Guinea. Once there, it fought dismounted and lacking a battalion of 155s.

As for the 2d, less its battalion of 105s[22], it reached Oran on March 9 1944, but was officially inactivated on 10 May, its elements being divided up between the Engineer Corps and Service units.

Another reorganization was planned for the 1st on 30 September 1944, reducing its manpower to 11,216 and its animals to 7,367. This however was obviously null and void, for at that date the 1st Cavalry had its own organization and operated as infantry. Then, on 20 July 1945, it was completely reorganized along Infantry lines, but retained the designation "Cavalry".

(National Archives)

THE ARTILLERY OF THE ARMORED DIVISIONS

The Armored Command's FM 17-100 Manual devoted to the Armored Division, 15 January 1944 version. (Private Collection)

*Top:
20 July 1943, passing by Scaccia on the southern coast of Sicily which was occupied the previous day, a howitzer trundles along in the direction of Palermo.*

AS IN the majority of armies worldwide, except for the German Army, the American armored forces were initially shared between the infantry and the cavalry, and struggled for recognition and consequently for the right to define an operational doctrine and equipment of their very own.

However, after the stunning German victories in Poland and then France, an armored larger unit was improvised out of the 7th Mechanized Cavalry Brigade at Fort Knox and the Provisional Tank Brigade at Fort Benning. At the close of the particularly successful maneuvers in Louisiana in 1940, on 10 July – sixteen days before the GHQ was activated – the War Department decided to activate the Armored Force under Brigadier General Adna R. Chaffee.

On 1 August 1941, he was succeeded by Major General Jacob L. Devers, and on 1 June 1942 the force came under the control of the AGF who set about drawing up an operational doctrine and supervising the training, organization and commissioning of the Armored units up to corps level. All its activities were concentrated at Fort Knox, Kentucky, including in particular the specialist committee charged with develo-

ping and testing equipment and tactics, ever since the Armored School had been created there in September 1940.

The armored division was the base element of the Armored Force, which featured a high degree of mobility, heavy firepower and shock tactics, augmented by its ability to conduct largely autonomous operations.

THE "HEAVY" ARMORED DIVISION

The first two divisions were activated on 15 July 1940:

— 1st Armored at Fort Knox based on the 7th Cavalry Brigade

— 2d Armored at Fort Benning with elements of the Provisional Tank Brigade.

The first of these took part in the maneuvers in Arkansas in August 1941, and then in those held in Louisiana in September and in the Carolinas in October-November. The second joined in the last two sets of maneuvers.

As defined on 15 November 1940, and largely inspired by the Panzerdivisionen, the armored division was a complete independent combined arms formation, capable of launching deep penetration attacks to reach key objectives in the enemy's rear areas. 12,697 men strong, it was composed of essentially an armored brigade of 368 tanks divided between two light regiments and one heavy, an artillery regiment, a reconnaissance battalion and an Air Corps observation squadron. Among its support echelons were an "armored" infantry regiment and a field artillery battalion.

Two new armored divisions were formed on 15 April 1941:
— 3d Armored at Camp Beauregard, Louisiana, which moved to California to train at the Desert Training Center until November 1942
— 4th Armored at Pine Camp, New York, which followed its predecessor to California.

Finally, on 1 October 1941, the 5th Armored was established at Fort Knox and joined the 3d in California.

Then on 1 March 1942 the new organization prepared by Armored Force was adopted, which validated the designation of the divisions as "heavy".

	Division	Artillery div
Officers	691	102
Warrant officers	69	9
Enlisted	13 432	2 016
Total	14 192	2 127
.50-cal Browning	103	24
75 mm Howitzers	68	30
105 mm Howitzers	54	54
Light Tanks	158	-
Medium Tanks	232	9
Half-Tracks	694	207
2 1/2 Trucks	422	75

Each one was now composed of two identical Regiments each made up of two battalions of light tanks and two of medium tanks. It also included an armored infantry regiment[1] of three battalions, plus three S-P 105 mm howitzer battalions under a divisional artillery commander[2].

Apart from its transition to a basically "triangular" structure, the innovative element was the creation of two command units designated "Combat Commands", each one commanded by a brigadier general. The division commander could delegate to a brigadier general the combined arms elements required to carry out a specific mission. Tactical teams could thus be assembled, their components varying according to the desired result.

THE "LIGHT" ARMORED DIVISION

The fortunes of the 1st Armored took a dive in its first head-on clash at the battle of Kasserine Pass in Tunisia. In two days it lost two battalions of tanks and most of its artillery, paying for the tactical inexperience of its units, who were lacking in combined arms training due to insufficient means and the results of hasty mobilization.

The excellent performance of the 68th Armored FA Battalion should however be noted. Completely cut off from friendly forces, it formed itself into a circle just like the covered wagon trains during the ope-

ning up of the American West, and at dusk threw back a tank attack some 2,000 yards to its rear. Then, in the dark it formed up into two columns protected on all four sides by an S-P 105 howitzer primed for action, and striking out westwards it succeeded in rejoining the American lines.

As a result, beginning in February 1943 new tables of organization, taking into account the experience gained in Tunisia and Sicily, were studied by the G-3

Gun crew at their posts: chief, aimer using the panoramic sight M12, loader just behind the angled sighting scope and his hand on the breech lever, second loader ready to load a round into the chamber

1-The French used the more appropriate designation of "portée" or "transported". The armored infantry differed from the foot infantry – who were not basically motorized – and from the proper motorized infantry – organized to be transported by truck – as all its personnel was carried in half-tracks.
2-Strength: 34 including six officers at the divisional artillery level; 736 including 37 officers and three warrant officers per battalion.

MAKEUP OF THE BATTALION OF S-P 105 HOWITZERS				
	HQ Battery T/O&E 6-166	Firing Batteries T/O&E 6-167	Service Battery T/O&E 6-169	Total IT/O&E 6-160
Officers	14	4	5	31
Warrant-officers	-	-	2	2
Enlisted	97	106	86	506
Total	111	110	93	534
Aircraft	2	-	2	2
105 mm Howitzer	-	6	-	18
.50 cal Browning	6	4	8	26
Rocket Launcher	11	7	8	40
81 mm mortars	-	-	2	2
Medium tanks	3	-	-	3
Half-Tracks M3A1	10	7	-	31
Jeeps	9	3	3	21
Command Cars	-	-	2	2
Dodge 4 x 4	-	-	1	1
GMC Trucks	1	1	21	25
1-ton trailers	2	2	12	20
M10 trailers	-	8	9	33
Wrecker	-	-	1	1
Tank Recovery T5	-	-	1	1

Distinctive unit insignia of the 27th FA Armored Battalion of the 1st Armored Division, which saw combat on 2 December 1942 at Tebourba, in the Medjerda Valley in Tunisia. (Le Poilu, Paris)

Tunic of a captain in the 68th Battalion of the 1st Armored Division. The ribbons are the Distinguished Unit Citation of the 68th for action in Tunisia, the American and European-African Campaigns and the Victory Medal. (Le Poilu, Paris)

of the General Staff, the AGF and the Armored Force – which became the Armored Command on 2 July 1943 – in cooperation with a team of officers of the 1st Armored then in Sicily with the 2d Armored. Published on 15 September, they did not upset the overall organization but instead introduced several improvements compared with the previous system.

In the new "light" division, the regiment disappeared and was replaced by the battalion, which thus

	Division	Div Arty
Officers	558	101
Warrant officers	51	6
Enlisted	10001	1516
Total	10610	1623
Light Aircraft	8	6
Rockets Lanchers	74	16
.50 cal Browning	404	78
75 mm How.	17	-
105 mm How.	54	54
Light tank	77	-
Medium tank (75)	168	9
Medium tank(105)	18	-
Jeeps	449	63
Half-Tracks	451	93
GMC Trucks	422	75

became the basic unit. Numbering three each of tanks, infantry and artillery, they could be reinforced as necessary by identical battalions drawn from the General Reserve.

Each battalion fitted smoothly into the overall scheme, thanks to a headquarters unit, which took care of administration, and a service unit to transport supplies and replacements from the Army depots

A "Combat Command Reserve" was set up with fewer personnel, and the tank battalion comprised a company of light tanks for reconnaissance, three companies of medium tanks and six medium tanks armed with 105 mm howitzers.

15 February 1942 saw the beginning of the activation of the 6th Armored at Fort Knox. It was the first to be organized from the start as a "light" armored division.

Eight further armored divisions between March

	T/O	June 1943	June 1944	June 1945
Divisional Arty	6-160	2,127	1,739	1660
S-P 105 mm Bn	6-125	465	506	490

and November 1942 and two in March and July 1943 also received the "light" designation.

Of the armored divisions – the 1st, 2d and 3d - which had gone into battle under the designation "heavy", only the 1st joined the 4th and 10th in converting to the new structure. The 2d and 3d Armored retained their original structure until the end of

the war.

A new series of T/O, published on 24 January 1945 made few changes, apart from the addition of nine Medium Tanks and an increase in total manpower to 10,670.

Just as in the division as a whole, the tendency was to reduce the Artillery theoretic strength.

THE SELF PROPELLED 105 MM HOWITZER BATTALION

All the modifications applied to the composition of the armored divisions were not without consequences for their artillery units. Thus on 1 January 1942, in the 1st Armored, the 68th Regiment of S-P 105s gave birth to the 68th Battalion, and the 27th Battalion of towed 105s was transformed into an armored unit. On 8 January the newly created 91st Battalion of S-P 105s was attached to it.

In the 2d Armored, the 14th Regiment was transformed into a battalion in the same manner as for the 68th while the 72d Armored Battalion, formed in July 1940, remained associated with the 92d, which was also attached to the 2d Armored.

The 3d and 4th Armored followed in the same way as the 1st, but with the 67th Regiment and the 54th and 391st Battalions for the former and the 66th Regiment and the 22nd and 94th Battalions for the latter.

In the 5th Armored, the 65th Regiment gave birth in the same fashion, on 1 January 1942, to the 65th Battalion, which passed into the General Reserve on 1 September, as did the 58th Battalion on 20 August. The 95th Battalion activated on 1 January, the 71st, which exchanged its 75 mm horse-drawn howitzers for S-P 105s on 1 September, and the 47th, which did the same on 9 September but with towed 105s, replaced them.

In the 6th Armored, its three battalions were replaced by three others during the months of September and October 1942.

Finally, the 9th Armored absorbed two battalions of horse-drawn 75s – the 16th Bn on 3 June and the 3d on 14 July – from the inactivated 2d Cavalry Division and the 73d Battalion of towed 105s on 15 July.

— Matters greatly improved from then on, each battalion being formed and assigned at the moment their own division was activated.

— Finally, the artillery of the armored division took on a different form to that of the infantry division. It certainly had a ternary structure, but a colonel, assisted by a lieutenant colonel, commanded it and it was made up of:

— a headquarters that could be reinforced, as the need arose, with vehicles and men by the divisional headquarters company

— three battalions of 105s (T/O&E 6-165).

Each battalion comprised a headquarters battery, three firing batteries and a service battery.

In addition, a medical detachment of 10 corpsmen commanded by a surgeon captain, with one Jeep fitted with an SCR 510 radio set and a M3 ambulance half-track with 1-ton trailer, would be attached to each battalion prior to taking ship for the European Theater

---

3-33 in the three chests under the front and rear floor, 24 in the lockers in the rear corners of the hull.

105 MM HOWITZER MOTOR CARRIAGE T19

(National Archives)

The US Army had experimented with several models of S-P gun during the 1920s and 30s, but the German successes of 1940 drove the Americans to adopt artillery pieces mounted on tracked chassis. However, bearing in mind the urgency of the situation, the easiest solution was to use a half-track vehicle such as the one already used for the antitank gun.

The combination of the M3 half-track and the 105 mm Howitzer M2A1 on Mounting T2, suggested in September 1941, was at first rejected. Then at the end of October it was approved using a modified chassis: alteration of the windshield to allow the barrel to depress, raised seats, gas tanks moved to the rear, and general strengthening following trials over difficult terrain. A gun shield similar to that used on the towed howitzer was then added, and the hull was strengthened to withstand high-angle fire.

The howitzer crew comprised seven (eventually eight) gunners, plus the two drivers for the half-track. A trailer could be towed.

The first production unit was delivered in January 1942, followed by 323 units constructed before production ended in April.

Conceived as a stopgap while awaiting the availability of superior fully tracked vehicles, the T19 was primarily used for training. However, a limited number saw action in North Africa and then in Sicily, in Italy and even during the invasion of Southern France although this type had been officially withdrawn from service in 1943.

The T19 was definitively struck from active service in July 1945 and the 90 remaining units were reconverted to personnel carriers M3A1.

SPECIFICATIONS

• Weight empty	18,012 pounds
• Weight in traveling order	21,495 pounds
• Overall length	19.7 ft
• Width	6.56 ft
• Height (without machine gun)	8.2 ft
• Armor thickness (shield & radiator)	0.25 inch at 25°
• Armor thickness (windshield)	0.50 inch
• Armor thickness (sides & rear)	0.25 inch
• Tire size	825x20
• Ground pressure	37 pounds/sq in
• Horizontal traverse	400 mils approx
• Per turn of the traversing handwheel	19 mils
• Elevation	-5° to +35°
• Per turn of the elevating handwheel	10 mils
• Ammunition carried	8 rounds of 105
• Secondary armament	.50-cal Browning machine gun
• Motor	White 160AX 6-cylinder 150 hp
• Power-to-Weight ratio	14.7 hp/ton
• Maximum road speed	44 mph at 3000 rpm
• Maximum incline	60
• Fording capacity	33 inches
• Obstacle clearing	12.2 inches
• Range 200 miles	

49

105 MM HOWITZER MOTOR CARRIAGE M7

Despite the fruitless experiments conducted during the Great War, the Westervelt Board recommended the continuation of tests to produce a 105 mm howitzer on caterpillar tracks. This was done, but no such equipment entered service prior to the outbreak of the Second World War.

In 1941, the requirements laid down by the Armored Force led to the construction of three different models, all based on the chassis of the Grant medium tank but differing according to specific missions:
- the antitank version armed with the 3-inch Gun Model 1918
- the antiaircraft version with the new 3-inch AA Gun M1
- the field artillery version with the 105 mm Howitzer M2.

When the last version was officially adopted in April 1942, it had already been in production for several months. The artillery had received their first examples and the British had already christened it the "Priest" on account of the shape of the .50-cal machine gun mounting which resembled a church pulpit.

- It was actually the gunners who first used it and

SPECIFICATIONS

• Weight empty	42,836 lb	• Sustained rate of fire	2 rounds/minute
• Weight in traveling order	46,540 lb	• Ammunition carried	57 rounds of 105 on the vehicle3
• Overall length	18.7 ft		42 rounds of 105 in the Trailer M8
• Width	8.85 ft		300 rounds of .50-cal
• Height (without machine gun)	8.2 ft	• Secondary armament	.50-cal Browning M2 HMG
• Ground pressure	13.5 pounds/sq in	• Motor	Wright R975C1
• Horizontal traverse	218 mils left, 453 mils right		9 cylinder air-cooled
• Per turn of the traversing handwheel	19 mils	• Maximum road speed	25 mph at 2,100 rpm
• Elevation	-90 to +580 mils	• Maximum incline	35
• Per turn of the elevating handwheel	10 mils	• Fording capacity	42 inches
• Rapid rate of fire	4 rounds/minute	• Range	143 miles

Distinctive insignia of the 68th Armored FA Bn coming from the regiment assigned to the 1st Armored Division in 1940.
(Le Poilu, Paris)

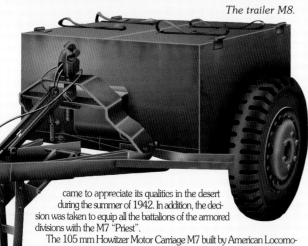

The trailer M8.

came to appreciate its qualities in the desert during the summer of 1942. In addition, the decision was taken to equip all the battalions of the armored divisions with the M7 "Priest".

The 105 mm Howitzer Motor Carriage M7 built by American Locomotive comprised a 105 mm Howitzer M2A1 on Mount M4 installed in the cut-down hull of the M3 Grant or the M4 Sherman medium tanks. The column length and the time to pass for each battery were 2,900 yards and 8 minutes by day. At night, the column spacing was halved.

I-n the M7 the crew composition and duties were similar to those in the T19. The driver was responsible for manning the .50-cal Browning machine gun. The gun chief would order the drivers to maneuver their vehicles, and when the ammunition half-track was involved in local defense, its driver would man his .50-cal.

he M7 could tow the armored ammunition trailer M8 that weighed slightly over one ton and could carry a load of 2,180 pounds (990 kg).

Right from the time it first saw combat in Tunisia in 1943, the M7 demonstrated its excellent capabilities thanks to the ability to open fire immediately after coming to a stop, or even on the move. More than 4,000 were finally built by February 1945, when the needs of the Army were fulfilled and two new versions were conceived: the M7 on the chassis of the M4 (3,314 built) and beginning in March 1944, the M7B1 on the chassis of the M4A3 (826 built).

(National Archives)

THE LIGHT AND MEDIUM ARTILLERY
OF THE GENERAL RESERVE

Enamelled insignia of the 142nd FA Group formed in February 1942 from the 142nd Arkansas National Guard Regiment and attached to VII Corps in Europe. (Coll. Le Poilu)

Top:
8 July 1944, the 155 HMIs of A Battery, 333rd Battalion (Colored) in position in the Valley of the Serres, supporting the attack by VIII Corps to the north of Périers.

U P UNTIL THE CREATION of the Army Ground Forces in March 1942, units not attached to specific divisions made up organic elements of large formations or belonged to the GHQ Reserve.

The "type" army consisted of three corps but had no artillery of its own and the "type" corps of three divisions and an artillery brigade with one regiment of guns and two regiments of 155 mm howitzers, plus an observation battalion. These two larger units were charged solely with planning, and for mobilizing and training the forces attached to them.

However, once the principles proposed by General McNair had been accepted by the War Department, this scheme was significantly modified. The basis of his reforms was that the armies and the corps should become made-to-measure command units, in other words they should be composed of the elements required to carry out a certain mission. As for the division, reinforced according to individual circumstances, they should not fight strictly according to their organizational tables, but in combined arms teams.

In 1943, the old brigades were disbanded and the regiments disappeared to form separate battalions, except in the Infantry. It was initially planned to create brigade headquarters, but except for the Antiaircraft Artillery where they

became the norm, they were not found to be necessary for the Field Artillery as their battalions were attached directly to the corps.

THE REFORMS OF 1943

The accent laid on attachment rather than assignment, the disappearance of organic elements from the armies and the corps, and the limitation of the division to those units strictly necessary, created a large pool of formations, which were not attached to individual divisions. Representing in fact the General Reserve, they functioned as organic elements as and when they were specifically allocated to an army or a corps. In the same spirit, in reality each division also belonged to the GHQ reserve, since they no longer belonged to a corps but were attached to one according to the operational requirement.

Accordingly, on 24 December 1942, the War Department authorized the transformation of the non-divisional regiments of mechanized cavalry, field and antiaircraft artilleries, and combat engineers, and the creation of group headquarters.

The combat formations were accordingly organized into separate battalions, being interchangeable elements of the smallest size compatible with the degree of combat efficiency required. Each army therefore became a combination of corps with additional separate battalions, and the corps a combination of divisions and battalions.

The group was a form of organization already adopted by

Distinctive unit insignia of the 13th FA Brigade, which fought in Italy in September 1943 having passed via England, Northwestern Africa and Sicily. (Le Poilu, Paris)

During the night of 29/30 January 1944 to the east of Cassino, a 155 mm howitzer of Battery B, 936th Battalion – formed one year earlier from a battalion of the 142nd Regiment – fires in support of the troops of II Corps.

1-For comparison, the AGF had only 250 officers to control 2,000,000 men.

certain new arms such as the tank and the antitank units. It possessed no T/O of its own, and the battalions did not constitute an integral part but were attached or detached according to operational requirements. The number of attached battalions was variable: sometimes none, normally four, eventually as many as six. The group was to be in overall command of these units during operations and be responsible for their specialized training. Each battalion's administrative needs were handled directly by the particular army, from whose depots they drew their supplies.

The conversion process was carried out progressively through the course of 1943. It took account not only of the disbanding of the regiments, but also the adjustments inside each battalion in order for them to effectively handle their own internal administration. And with the growth in the number of groups attached directly to the corps, fewer brigades were found to be necessary. Their dissolution allowed the activation of headquarters batteries in each of the corps.

The other objective of the reforms set in motion by General McNair was to reduce the size of the staffs. The replacement of the regiments by groups would save manpower but also speed up the pace of operations. Out of the total number of Army officers in 1943, only one in fifty was a long service career officer. Many of these were assigned to staffs, some of which had grown to a significant size[1] and whose overall effect was to slow down the pace of operations.

One solution was to combine the roles of commandment and administration on the lines of the structure adopted in the divisional artilleries. On the other hand, as a flexible organizational structure increasingly became the standard, the work of the army and corps staff continued to expand in order to cope.

Between 1943 and 1945, the theoretical strengths of the various headquarters batteries evolved as per the following table:

At the same time, the formation of new brigades to head up the groups was also envisaged. The brigades would comprise only a command element to which a number of formations would be attached, varying as per the requirement of the time.

	T/O	06/1943	06/1944	06/1945
Corps Arty (Mot.)	6-50-1	97	116	112
FA Brigade (Mot.)	6-20-1	111	103	107
FA Group (Mot.)	6-12	-	99	99
Amd Arty Group	6-12	96	-	-

CORPS, BRIGADES AND GROUPS

The majority of the brigade headquarters batteries gave birth to equivalent units for the corps artillery, either in the United States prior to posting overseas, or in situ in the theaters of operations. Similarly, certain corps batteries were either formed from groups or regiments, or were created from scratch:

	Activation		Brigade	TO
VIII	09.08.43	USA	72d (NG)	NW Europe
XIII	10.08.43	USA	15th	NW Europe
XII	11 08 43	USA	22d	NW Europe
XI	14.08.43	USA	19th	Pacific
XV	17.08.43	USA	16th	NW Europe
III	18.08.43	USA	14th	NW Europe
IV	18.08.43	USA	75th (NG)	Italy
IX	30.08.43	USA	74th (NG)	Pacific
X	01.09.43	USA	73rd (NG)	Pacific
XIX	10.10.43	USA	141st	NW Europe
VI	10.12.43	Italy	18th	Italy, NWE
XXI	29.12.43	USA	112th	NW Europe
V	14.02.44	England	76th(NG)	NW Europe
II	12.03.44	Italy	71(NG)	Italy
VII	13.03.44	England	17th	NW Europe

Out of the eight remaining brigades, the 26th activated in June 1941 was sent to Java via Australia, from where it returned in March 1942 to be inactivated at the beginning of July.

	Activation		Brigade	TO
XX	21.10.43	USA	-	NW Europe
XIV	11.43	Guadalcanal	-	Pacific
XVI	10.12.43	USA	172d Gp	NW Europe
XXII	15.01.44	USA	-	NW Europe
XXIII	15.01.44	USA	-	NW Europe
I	18.01.44	Australia	147th Regt	Pacific
XXIV	31.05.44	Hawaii	225th Gp	Pacific
XXXVI	10.07.44	USA	-	-
XXXII	17.10.04	USA	427th Gp	-

The 31st remained at Fort Sill between December 1943 and February 1945, and the 46th (Colored) activated in Louisiana in February 1941 became a group in September 1943 and disappeared from the lists on 31 January 1944.

Three landed in France on 18 and 27 August 1944 via England:

— the 34th formed in March 1944 with the headquarters battery of the 181st Group

— the 32d formed in February 1944 and the 33rd in March with the headquarters batteries of the 403d and 166th Groups respectively. The 61st was formed in July 1944 with the 222d Group, arrived directly in France on 21 January 1945 and entered Germany on 6 April.

Finally, the most famous was the 13th Brigade attached

Distinctive unit insignia of the 17th FA Battalion formed in Pozzili in March 1944 out of the 1st Battalion of the 17th Regiment and equipped with 155 mm Howitzers M1. (Le Poilu, Paris)

On 14 August 1943, some 20 miles from Messina, landing craft delivered a battery of 155 mm Howitzers M1918 onto the beach at Patti

2-For convenience, the term "Group" is used here instead of the full designation of "HHB, FA Group".
3-10 saw combat in Italy, 59 in France and 9 in the Pacific.
4-Formed at Fort Sill on 8 Feb 43 with the 1st Bn, 196th FA Regiment, arrived in France 8 Jul 44.

pre-war to I Corps at Fort Bragg. Transiting by way of England, it arrived in North Africa on 5 December 1942 but only moved to Italy via Sicily on 21 September 1943. It was transferred to the French Expeditionary Corps on its arrival in the Abruzzi Mountains and played a crucial role in the Battle of the Garigliano. Next it landed in Southern France, and left the French 2d Corps – in which it formed the heavy artillery component – at the end of hostilities only.

The groups[2], usually formed from the regiment whose number they bore, eventually came to total 101.

Inspired by the tank groups activated in February 1942, two armored artillery groups were formed in September 1942, but they lost their "armored" designation during the following year: the 5th in England on 14 August and the 6th in Italy on 10 December.

Sixty other groups were activated in 1943 and a further 39 in 1944, several ultimately giving birth, as noted above, to a brigade or a corps artillery, and 79 participated in combat operations[3]. Out of their total number, three were formed out of antiaircraft formations, including the 48th (Colored), which was set up on 31 December 1944 in Marseille with the elements of the 8th Antiaircraft Artillery Group, which had arrived from Italy on 24 November.

FIELD ARTILLERY BATTALIONS
(75 MM PACK HOWITZER)

Even if the 75 mm and 105 mm howitzer units formed the basis of the divisional artilleries, not all of them were thus employed.

Among the battalions of 75s, we find the 98th activated in January 1941 at Fort Lewis, Washington. Taking ship at Hampton Roads on 27 December 1942, it passed through the Panama Canal and reached Australia in January 1943. It underwent training with a view to a landing in the Philippines, and then from 26 August 1944 it fought in New Guinea. It was there that on 24 September it became the 6th

Rangers Battalion, and one month later it covered and preceded the major landings in Elite Gulf. It would seem that the shortage of pack animals and the problems of using them in the jungles of the Southwest Pacific Area were the underlying reasons for this change of plan. Actually, the sole battery of the 603d Battalion, activated in the port of Charleston in February 1942, was disbanded on Guadalcanal in October 1943.

On the other hand, two of the four battalions activated in December 1943 at Camp Gruber, Oklahoma, fought in Burma, the 612th from August 1944 and the 313th from November. But the 610th and 611th, remaining in the USA, were both inactivated, in July 1944 at Camp Carson, Colorado in the case of the former and in February 1945 at Fort Riley, Kansas for the latter.

Finally, two battalions specially trained for mountain operations – the 601st activated at Fort Bragg in April 1942 and the 602d activated at Camp Carson in July – spent time in Alaska from August to November 1943 before taking ship in Seattle for Hampton Roads in Virginia. Having reached Italy by way of North Africa in March 1944, they operated with II Corps. Designated as FA Battalions (Mountain) by the Fifth Army, up until their departure for France they were supported by a specially assembled troop of trucks. Then the 602d, reorganized as a glider pack howitzer battalion was attached to the First Airborne Task Force, as a part of which it took part in the glider assault in Province. As for the 601st, it reached France on 15 October.

With the airborne forces, the 462d Parachute Battalion that was activated at Camp Mack all, North Carolina in June 1943 reached Australia on 29 March 1944. Along with the 503d Parachute Infantry it formed a regimental combat team, which jumped over the Isle of Noemfoor on 3 July before reaching the Philippines in November. Finally, two battalions served solely in the Continental United States. The 215th (Glider) Battalion activated in January 1943 at Fort Bragg had only a brief existence, its 75s being replaced by

Distinctive unit insignia of the 4th FA Battalion, inherited from the 4th Regiment. (Collection of Le Poilu)

On 2 February 1944 in the Anzio beachhead, while VI Corps was on the defensive, the crew of a 105 M7 of the 69th Armored FA Battalion makes good use of the lull in the fighting.

(National Archives)

Sack for bagged charge for the 8-inch howitzer, and sack plus additional bag charges for the 105 mm Howitzer M2. (Private Collection)

155s one year later. And the 467th Parachute Battalion, after several months spent at Camp Mackall between March and July 1944, was reformed in December as a display unit at the Airborne Training Center, the last remnant of the Airborne Command, in February 1944.

FIELD ARTILLERY BATTALIONS
(105 MM HOWITZER)

It was the same for the 105 Battalions, several separate battalions of which being primarily designated as reinforcements for divisions dedicated to specific operations. The 4th Infantry Division, for example, was reinforced on several occasions in 1944 during the campaign in France by the 105 mm howitzers of the 196th Battalion[4]:

— between 11 and 13 August, during the counter-attack to the south of Mortain

— from 13 to 23 October, when they broke through the Siegfried Line

— from 9 November to 2 December, during the counter-attack to break through to the forces surrounded in the Huertgen Forest.

— The armored larger units made use of the separate battalions as well, for example the 2d Armored Division, which on eleven occasions was reinforced by one, and sometimes two battalions of S-P 105s.

— The attachment of battalions of the General Reserve to divisional battalions, or the reinforcement of divisional firepower, was made easier because the former were set up along similar lines. They had the same organization and the same equipment, which solved any possible problems of integrating them into the radio networks and taking part in the fire plans and the logistic support.

— One fifth of all the 105 mm howitzer battalions were allocated to the General Reserve: one formed in 1940, 17 in 1942, 21 in 1943 and 12 in 1944. Out of these 51 battalions, 6 (five tractor-drawn) served in the Pacific and 37 in France.

— In Italy, where the terrain was very broken up and difficult, the 105 mm Howitzer M2 was not popular, because of its lack of effectiveness against a dug-in and protected enemy. The only unit used there was the 522d Battalion, activated on 1 February 1943 at Camp Shelby, Missouri, with Americans of Japanese origin, just like the 442d Infantry Regiment (Nisei), with which it formed the 442d RCT. They arrived in Italy on 28 May 1944, one week before the fall of Rome. It then reached France at the end of September, and fought in the region around Bruyères in October.

The 97th Battalion (Tractor-Drawn) was the sole battalion of the GHQ Reserve which fought in the Pacific. Formed on 4 January 1941 at Fort Bragg, North Carolina, it exchanged its 75 mm pack howitzers for 105s in 1942, shortly before leaving for New Caledonia in March.

After a tour of duty in Guadalcanal between January and

*Tunic of a captain of the 97th FA Battalion with the shoulder patch of the Tenth Army to the right (hidden in this photo) and of the US Army Forces, Pacific Ocean Area to the left. The 105 mm Howitzers M2 of the 97th fought on Guadalcanal in January 1943.
(Le Poilu, Paris)*

December 1943, it reached the Philippines on 21 May 1945. Six Battalions remained in United States:

— he 393d remained in Texas from April 1944 to March 1945

— the 1114th served in Panama, Puerto Rico and Hawaii from July 1944 to August 1945

— the 566th, at Fort Sill from April 1944 to February 1945, seems to have acted as display troop after the transformation and departure for Europe of the battalions of the 18th FA, the traditional display regiment of the School of Artillery

— the 424th, formed at the same time at Fort Riley, Kansas, and assigned to the Replacement & School Command from November 1944 to February 1945

— the 636th also formed in April 1944 but at Fort Sill and assigned to the Replacement & School Command in a similar fashion

— the 798th created at Fort Bragg in April 1944 and attached to the Field Artillery Board between May 1944 and March 1945.

One should also note the 689th Battalion activated on 8 February 1943 with the disbanding of the 18th Regiment of the School, and which reached England, to eventually land in France on 22 August 1944.

Finally, the 244th Battalion (Captured Weapons) deserves a special mention. Formed in August 1942, initially equipped with towed 105 mm howitzers, it then re-equipped with towed 155s. It reached England in July 1944 and landed in France on 31 July. During the advance eastwards, as the occasion arose it was charged with recovering and reusing the artillery pieces – 8,8 cm, 10 cm, 15 cm and 155 mm Schneider – and the ammunition abandoned by the Germans.

ARMORED FIELD ARTILLERY BATTALIONS

The same situation held true for the self-propelled 105 mm howitzer, the quality and availability of which were greatly appreciated during hard-fought actions or landings, as well as for their close support during advanced reconnaissance missions. Out of the 72 Battalions eventually formed, one third were included in the General Reserve.

Formed in February 1941 at Fort Bliss, Texas, in August 1942 the 62d Battalion exchanged its 105 mm Howitzers M2 for M7s, and thus became the first armored battalion to be attached to the General Reserve and also the first to be sent overseas, arriving in Morocco on 11 November 1942. It was followed by the 58th and 65th Battalions, activated at Fort Knox, Kentucky, in 1941 and released from their assignment to the 5th Armored Division in September 1942. The 62d and 65th Battalions which were attached to the 5th FA Armored Group – itself also formed in September 1942 but in California – went on to distinguish themselves in action with the elements of the 1st Armored Division during the attack on El Guettar in March 1943.

In Sicily, a battery of the 62d landed on 10 July with the first waves of the 3d Infantry Division. Alongside it during the assault phase was the 10th Divisional Battalion equipped with M7s. Thanks to their mobility, the S-P 105s rapidly landed and took up a position less than 1,000 yards from the shoreline to support the advance of the infantry. Before leaving Bizerte, Major General Lucian K. Truscott, the division commander, had decided to exchange the towed 105s for the machines of the 5th

Armored Artillery Group, to assist during the assault. After the remainder of the 62d had rejoined them that afternoon, the battalion, joining up with the 14th Battalion of the 2d Armored Division, participated in the capture of Canicatti[5] on 12 July.

The three battalions – the 59th, 69th and 93d – taken from the 6th Armored Division reached Italy on 23 October 1943, passing by way of North Africa. They next participated in the Dragoon operation on 15 August 1944, each one being attached to an assaulting infantry division: the 69th with the 3d at Cavalaire, the 59th with the 45th at Sainte-Maxime and the 93d with the 36th at Saint-Raphaël. Then when Task Force Butler was being assembled at Le Muy to push forward in the direction of the Durance and Grenoble, it included the 59th in support of a mechanized cavalry squadron, two tank companies and a battalion of motorized infantry.

The 5th Group became officially a Field Artillery Group (Motorized) on 14 August 1943. However, it was under its former designation that, as part of VIII Corps, it took part in the Normandy operation with three armored battalions. At Omaha Beach, the 62d and 58th landed on 6 June in direct support of the leading elements of the 1st and 29th Infantry Divisions. And at Utah Beach, the 65th landed with the 4th Infantry Division, its three light battalions being equipped with M7s, and joined the 101st Airborne Division when contact was made with the latter. It was followed by the 87th which took ship alongside the gunners of the two airborne divisions and who were landed on 9 June after the junction was effected with the 82d Airborne.

Equipped with the M7 from its formation at Fort Knox in April 1943, the 400th Battalion moved to England and landed in France on 17 July 1944. Eight days later the 83d followed, having exchanged its 105 mm Howitzers M2 for M7s in October 1942.

The 695th and 696th were formed in May 1943 at Fort Jackson, South Carolina, from elements of the 112th Regiment of the New Jersey National Guard, the remainder of the latter unit becoming a group. Converted to armor on 26 August, they reached England in February 1944 before landing in France in July.

Five other battalions were formed from towed 155 mm units:

— the 342d originally came from the 89th Infantry Division, converted in September 1943, and fought in Italy from 18 October 1944, then in France from 7 December

— the 253d, which converted in January 1944, left New York on 2 July and arrived in France on 19 August

— the 274th, 275th and 276th converted in February 1944 and which arrived in France by way of England on 19 August, 6 September and 24 August respectively.

They were followed by four battalions established on 25 March 1944 with battalions of tank destroyers activated at Camp Bowie, Texas:

— the 425th with the 650th TD Bn, which remained at Fort Knox

— the 426th, 427th and 428th with the 663d, 666th and 668th TD Bns respectively, which arrived in the Philippines via Hawaii too late to join combat.

In Italy, as was noted earlier in connection with the 10th Mountain Division, it was the antiaircraft artillery units that were used to form the 1125th at Naples on 25 September 1944.

Finally, between September 1943 and June 1944 the 262d served at the School of Artillery at Fort Sill as a towed 105 unit, first with trucks then with caterpillar tractors, before being converted onto S-P M7s in November. And two battalions of coast defense artillery transformed into the 783d

5. More than 2,500 105 mm shells obliterated 5-The town: 1,862 fired by the 14th and 607 by the 62d.

4.5-INCH GUN M1, CARRIAGE M1A1

The medium artillery included sixteen battalions armed with the 4.5-inch Gun (114 mm), operating in the European theater at corps level. This modest deployment was the result of lengthy production delays and the basic opposition of the AGF to a gun that, falling between the popular calibers of 105 mm and 155 mm, went against their attempt at standardization. A 4.7-inch caliber gun dating from 1906 had seen service during the World War I, and the Westervelt Board favored its continued development. Two projects were started, in 1920 and 1922, but were not proceeded with. Then in 1939 the model was revised and resulted in the 4.7-inch Gun T3, sharing a common mounting with the 155 mm howitzer M1. However, it was the 155 that went into production in January 1940.

With the war in Europe continuing, the gunners proposed a revised caliber of 4.5-inch, which would be compatible with current British ammunition. Thus modified, in April 1941 the 4.5-inch gun was accepted for service with the same mounting as the 155 Howitzer M1. The two pieces were very similar in appearance but its longer barrel could differentiate the 4.5-inch. Production started in September 1942 and finished in February 1944 after 416 guns had been built.

The first seven battalions[7], whose structure was similar to those armed with the 155 mm howitzer, were formed in April and May 1943. Six were sent to England in July 1944 and landed in France between 21 and 30 August 21. The seventh arrived one month later.

Five others, converted from National Guard Regiments, exchanged their 155 howitzers for 4.5-inch guns as follows:

— the 935th (Louisiana) and the 939th (Pennsylvania) before taking ship for North Africa in August. From there they were committed in Italy in October, before moving to France a year later

— the 959th (Tennessee), the 172d and 941st (New Hampshire) were re-equipped at the end of 1943 and went into combat in Normandy between 14 and 24 June 1944.

Then in 1944, the 259th and three battalions of the National Guard – 176th (Pennsylvania), 199th (New Jersey), 211th (Massachusetts) – armed with the 105 mm howitzer converted to the 4.5-inch Gun and landed in France in August and September. In the opposite direction, the 433d and the 429th formed in September/October 1944, handed in their 4.5-inch guns in exchange for 155 mm howitzers prior to taking ship for the Philippines in the summer of 1945.

Not liked by its users, the 4.5-inch was finally withdrawn in 1945, because the performance of its ammunition was inferior to that of the 155 and its non-standardized caliber caused logistical problems.

1-The 770th, 771st, 772d, 773d at Camp Bowie, Texas, and the 774th, 775th, 777th (Colored) at Camp Beale, California.

• Weight in traveling order	24,690 lb
• Overall length 26.7 ft • Height	6.96 ft
• Length of barrel	16.4 ft
• Width across the tires	7.9 ft
• Traverse	53°
• Maximum elevation	65°
• Rapid rate of fire	4 rounds per minute
• Sustained rate of fire	1 round per minute
• Muzzle velocity	2,274 ft/sec
• Time for positioning	5 minutes

and 784th and equipped with 8-inch Guns in August 1944, finally became Armored in February 1945 but remained in the United States.

FIELD ARTILLERY BATTALIONS
(155 MM HOWITZER)

Out of the 177 battalions of towed 155 howitzers activated between 1940 and 1945, 111 belonged to the General Reserve and all except four used tractors as tow vehicles. They were capable of rapidly reinforcing the supporting artillery of a large infantry formation, but they were more often attached to heavy artillery units and made up groups at corps level.

Shortly after the attack on Pearl Harbor, the 81st Battalion was formed on 18 December 1940 at Fort Lewis, Washington, from the regiment created five months earlier. After a tour of duty in Alaska, it returned to take ship in New York for England, and arrived in France on 2 October 1944.

Two others were activated in January 1941, plus another at the end of that year:
— the 2d in Panama from a battalion of the 22d Regiment, sent to England in July 1944 and that landed in France on 16 August
— the 4th at Fort Bragg from a 75 mm pack howitzer battalion, which left for the New Hebrides in May 1942 and finished the war in the Philippines
— the 75th from a battalion of towed 75 mm guns formerly part of the 7th Division, which after a tour of duty in Alaska arrived in Italy on 7 April 1945.

Next, between February and June 1942 the 154th, 198th and 145th Battalions of the National Guard were activated, originally with towed 75 mm guns. And the 209th, activated at Fort Lewis on 1 April, after a tour of duty in Alaska, landed in France in March 1945.

In 1943, fifty-six battalions were activated, including 21 belonging to the National Guard, the majority using trucks as tow vehicles, which were replaced by caterpillar tractors often at the last minute before taking ship for overseas.

Among the battalions which from November 1943 fought in Italy, having transited by way of Northwestern Africa, featured the 141st, 933d and 937th which then moved to Italy and France. The first mission of the 933d was to reinforce the artillery of the 2d Moroccan Infantry Division, which it continued to support in the Garigliano bridgehead. And the 141st and 937th landed in Southern France on 15 August 1944, the former with VI Corps and the latter with the 36th Infantry Division at Saint-Raphael.

Also fighting alongside French units was the 178th Regiment of the South Carolina National Guard, which arrived in Italy in September 1943 from Sicily, and was attached to the 13th Brigade. On 24 February 1944, when stationed in the Abruzzi Mountains, it was disbanded as part of the general reorganization scheme, to form the 178th Group with the 178th and 248th Battalions at Venafro and San Elia respectively. The 17th Regiment followed it to the 13th Brigade a month later. Then it was also disbanded on 1 March 1944 and redesignated the 17th Group and the 17th and 630th Battalions on 1 March at Pozzili and on 24 February at Viticuso respectively.

Finally, two other Regiments supported American troops in Italy. The 36th, which arrived in September 1943 via Tunisia and Sicily, was disbanded on 5 March 1944 to form the 36th Group and two battalions:
— the 36th at Nettuno, in the Anzio bridgehead, that landed with VI Corps in Southern France on 15 August
— the 633d at Mignano, near Cassino, which remained in Italy.

As for the 77th that arrived in Italy also by way of Tunisia and Sicily at the end of October, it became a group on 24 February 1944 and formed the 631st at Cassino and the 634th at Anzio, which then landed in Southern France on 16 August. Up until the end of 1943 around forty battalions were formed, often out of inactivated regiments, and mostly destined for the European theater. Immediately behind the 5th Group, fourteen of these constituted the second echelon of the First Army on the Normandy beaches. There the 155 mm Howitzers M1 of the 953d and 955th Battalions of the National Guard were landed on 16 June on Omaha Beach.

Five battalions formed in 1943 changed their original equipment for 155 howitzers M1 in the following year. The 215th handed in its 75 mm pack howitzers in January and arrived in France in December. The 55th and 165th destined for the Pacific, and the 254th and 257th which arrived in Europe towards the war's end, had all originally been equipped with the 105 mm Howitzer M2.

On 1 April 1943 at Camp Livingstone, Louisiana, the 350th and 351st Regiments (Motorized) with 155 mm guns formed the 350th and 351st FA groups plus four separate battalions equipped up until November 1944 with towed 105s, and from that date onward with 155 mm Howitzers M1 and caterpillar tractors:
— the 350th and 351st formed from the 1st Bns of the 350th and 351st Regiments respectively fought in Europe from the end of February 1945
— the 971st and 973d formed from the 2d Bns of the same Regiments remained in the United States.

Elsewhere, the eight battalions (colored) also underwent modification. Thus the 349th Regiment attached to the

(National Archives)

Replacement and School Command at Fort Sill, Oklahoma, gave birth on 12 February 1943 to the 349th FA Group and to two battalions that fought in Europe from the beginning of February 1945:
— the 349th formed out of the 1st Bn of the original motorized 155 mm gun regiment, and the 686th formed from the 2d Bn with towed 75 mm Guns, which were both equipped with 105s up until 1944, and with 155 mm Howitzers M1 and full-track tractors thereafter.

Finally, the 184th Regiment, mobilized in Chicago in January 1941 as part of the Illinois National Guard, on 16 January 1943 formed the 930th and 931st which retained their towed 155s before being transformed in May 1944 in North Carolina and Georgia respectively, into combat engineer battalions.

Between March and October 1944, thirty other battalions were formed. Among these, the 433d and 429th, formed with 4.5-inch guns in September and October respectively, converted to 155 mm Howitzers M1 in 1945 prior to arriving in the Philippines.

"On 23 May 1944, VI Corps went over to the attack so as to get out of the Anzio beach-head. Moving along the Mussolini Canal in the direction of Cisterna, the 1st Special Service Force is being supported by the 463rd Parachute FA Bn of the Fifth Army. At 1st Regiment's HQ a forward observer is asking for supporting fire using an SCR 509 to help the infantry. Created from part of the personnel and materiel of the 456th sent to Great Britain, the group only had three 75 M1A1 howitzer pack batteries."

(National Archives)

THE HEAVY ARTILLERY
OF THE GENERAL RESERVE

O NE YEAR AFTER the declaration of war it appeared that the scope of the operations necessary to defeat the Axis powers might exceed the manpower and equipment capacity of the United States. Difficult choices would therefore have to be made at political and military levels:

- between the Navy which was fighting Japan in the Pacific and the Army which had landed in Africa and now waited in England to land on the Continent of Europe
- between the ground forces that won battles and occupied territory, and the air forces that wanted to win superiority in the skies
- between national interests and those of the Allies
- between the classic type of warfare and the B-29 four-engine bomber program, which was using up more and more resources. One of the questions to be resolved inside the Army was the relative importance of medium compared with heavy

artillery, and the relationship between the general reserve and the number of divisions.

From September 1942 the Army Ground Forces began to make it known that a significant increase in heavy artillery was necessary to create a balanced force. The AGF therefore recommended the creation of 140 heavy battalions in addition to 101 medium battalions and the divisional artillery units. The War Department first rejected this plan, and then reduced the number of medium battalions to 81, while authorizing the creation of 54. However, on 14 April 1943, the mobilization procedures were revised by the WD on the lines proposed by the AGF, taking into account the fact that there would be a pool of manpower (1,500,000 men) waiting to be employed overseas. The main readjustments they suggested concerned principally the abandonment of 38 antitank battalions and 118 antiaircraft battalions, and the addition of 32 battalions of medium and heavy artillery.

THE PROBLEM OF HEAVY ARTILLERY

General McNair felt that this latter number was dangerously inadequate if large-scale operations were to be undertaken before January 1945. After talks with Lieutenant General Brehon B. Sommervell, commanding the Army Service Forces, who was of the same opinion, he proposed an increase.

But the WD was reluctant to acquiesce, apparently believing

Tunic of a corporal of the 174th FA Battalion with the shoulder patch of VIII Corps and five overseas service stripes on the left sleeve. (Le Poilu, Paris)

Shoulder patch
of the General
Headquarters Reserve.
(Private Collection)

On 26 July 1944, V Corps
attacked to the east of St-Lo
with powerful artillery
support, including this
155 mm gun.

*Right: A gunner on a
155 mm Gun, 13 February
13 1944 at Nettuno.*

In First Army's sector, a
battery of 8-inch guns with
HST M4 moves into its
firing position.

(National Archives)

(National Archives)

	155 How	155 Gun	8-in How	8-in Gun	240 How	Total
1942						
30 Sep - recommended by AGF for 114 Divs	120	72	16	4	9	24
24 Nov - approved by WD for 100 Divs	65	40	6	4	4	135
31 Dec - 73 Divisions	53	24	6	-	3	85
1943						
14 Apr - recommended by AGF for 99 Divs	69	48	8	4	12	167
4 Oct - approved by WD for 90 Divs	66	40	19	-	12	149
28 Oct - WD Project for 105 Divs	80	50	19	-	12	173
31 Dec - 90 Divisions	63	34	17	-	10	163
1944						
15 Jan - approved by WD for 90 Divs	95	48	42	6	15	222
30 Jun - 89 Divisions	96	52	42	7	15	228
4 Oct - approved by WD for 89 Divs	96	48	64	8	23	257

that bombers could fulfil the mission of the heavy artillery.

McNair for his part remained unconvinced. Already in March 1941 he had explained his point of view in an exchange of notes with the G-2 of the WD, who felt that the air force/armor combination employed by the Germans could have rendered the traditional partnership of infantry/artillery obsolete. He doubted that the Army Air Force could replace the Field Artillery, while conceding that it would be useful in extending the depth of an attack.

The following table shows the growth in the mobilization of non-divisional battalions:

	31 Dec 42	30 Apr 43	Post-1943
Light Battalions	57	76	19
Medium Battalions	53	113	60
Heavy Battalions	32	137	105
Total	142	326	184

On 1 July 1943, an increase from 54 to 77 battalions was authorized. Then the program of tank destroyers was abandoned on 4 October, while that of the field artillery was decreased, but the formation of new units carried on in the meantime. But at the end of January 1944, only around sixty had been

155 MM GUN M1, CARRIAGE M1A1

During the Great War, the Field Artillery gained experience of mobile heavy artillery with the French 155 mm Gun GPF (Grande Puissance Filloux) and the British 8-inch Vickers Howitzer, issued in 1917 and coupled to a Caterpillar tractor. Because the Vickers model had insufficient range and accuracy, the GPF was the piece which was retained at the end of the war. However, the Westervelt Board recommended that design studies should be undertaken on a long-range gun and a mounting capable of taking either a 155 or a 203 to simplify production and reduce maintenance costs.

Several prototypes were produced during the 1920s and the 1930s.

However, due to a lack, of funds and the fact that a number of GPF Guns were available[1], it was not until 1938 that the 155 mm Gun type T4 on Carriage T2 was adopted under the designation 155 mm Gun M1 on Carriage M1.

Production started in October 1940. Then deliveries of the M1A1 version began in June 1941 with an improved breech mechanism. Following further modifications, the M2 was standardized in March 1945. As for the mounting which was common to both

activated, with some only just beginning their period of training. Again, once the requirements for 1944 had been circulated, the AGF went on the offensive once more, convinced that the overseas theater commanders had underestimated the sheer quantity of Heavy Artillery required to support a major offensive. The WD therefore authorized 30 additional heavy battalions, for a total of 111. Moreover, since the overall number of divisions had reduced, the ideal balance between divisions and medium/heavy Battalions sought by the AGF was actually achieved in July.

Finally, as a result of the fierce fighting around Cassino, the WD agreed a larger increase in the number of heavy artillery units than had initially been proposed by the AGF see on (left).

The following table shows how the heavy artillery program evolved between 1942 and 1944, in terms of the number of non-divisional battalions as proposed and approved[1].

As with all the artillery formations, the heavy battalions were split up into five batteries (headquarters, service and three firing batteries), their personnel, armament and vehicle establishment varying to suit the type of ordnance (right).

1- From Robert R. Palmer in Mobilization of the Ground Army in The Organization of Ground Combat Troops.

	155 Gun Truck-D[1]	155 Gun S-P[2]	8 How Truck-D[3]	8 Gun/ 240 How Tractor[4]
Officers	26	26	26	26
Warrant-officers	2	2	2	2
Enlisted	529	478	553	462
Total	557	506	581	490
Aircraft	2	2	2	2
Artillery pieces	12	12	12	6
.50-cal MG	19	19	19	19
Bazookas	34	34	34	28
Cargo trucks	-	12	-	12
Heavy tractors	-	-	-	18
Heavy wreckers	1	1	1	1
Mack tractors	18	-	18	-
GMC trucks	13	19	13	13
Command Cars	7	7	7	7
Dodge 4x4 armed	25	25	25	25
Jeeps	12	12	12	12
Crane trucks	-	-	-	3

Distinctive unit insignia of the 634th FA Battalion (77th Group) formed with 155 mm guns in February 1944 in Nettuno. (Private Collection)

1-T/O 6-55 dated 31 Jul 43.
2-T/O 6-155 dated 19 Sep 43. (See Gawne 1944, The Americans in Brittany p. 84).
3-T/O 66-395 dated 18 Aug 43. (See Gawne 1944, The Americans in Brittany p. 80).

the 155 mm gun and the 8-inch howitzer, from 1940 it was carried on pneumatic tires. In March 1944 a new fore-carriage was adopted which reduced the time needed to emplace the gun.

More than 4,000 guns were produced, 19 in 1942, 1,469 in 1943, 1,949 in 1944 and 598 in 1945. Under the Lend-Lease Act, 184 M1A1s were delivered to Great Britain and 25 to France[1].

The M1 or M1A1 Gun was made up of:
- the 155 mm barrel M1 or M1A1 (9,595 pounds / 4,352 kg)
- the 155 mm mounting M1 or M1A1 (20,305 pounds / 9,210 kg)
- the large-caliber fore-carriage M2 (1,975 pounds / 896 kg)
- the 155 mm gun recoil brake mechanism M3.

The 15-man crew – chief, four drivers and assistant drivers and 10 gunners – plus the ammunition were initially transported in two Mack NO-2 7¼-ton trucks, a 6x6 with tandem rear axles and a winch. Then the trucks were progressively replaced by full-tracked M4 HSTs (High-Speed Tractors) armed with a .50-cal Browning machine gun.

1-The 155 mm Gun M1917, 1917A1 or 1918 served up until 1942 in twelve motorized regiments – including six from the National Guard – normally attached to Corps. And under the Lend-Lease arrangement, 54 were ceded to the British and 48 to the French.

	T/O	June 1943	June 1944	June 1945
Truck-drawn	6-55	686	557	533
Tractor-drawn	6-355	-	562	541

Depending on the different versions, the battalion strengths were as above.

The "Long Tom", as it was nicknamed by the American artillerymen, was the mainstay of the corps artilleries and soon became the most popular and the most effective of the heavy ordnance pieces. Because of its carriage with 10 tires, it was featured on a poster celebrating war production entitled "Defense needs rubber!". 42 battalions were equipped with this gun between 1942 and 1945.

SPECIFICATIONS

- Weight in traveling order — 28,440 pounds tractor-drawn / 33,731 pounds truck-drawn
- Overall length — 34.4 ft
- Barrel length — 23 ft
- Caliber — L/45
- Height — 8.5 ft
- Width of the wheeled carriage — 8.2 ft
- Weight of the wheeled carriage — 5,380 pounds
- Traverse — 1,000 mils
- Elevation — 593 mils
- Max recoil at 0° — 5.4 ft approx
- Max recoil at 63° — 2.75 ft approx
- Average rate of fire — 1 round per minute (up to 10 rounds)
- Sustained rate of fire — 1 round every 2 minutes
- Maximum range — 25,040 yards
- Practical range — 20,122 yards
- Muzzle velocity — 2,800 ft/sec
- Time for positioning — 1 to 6 hours

A M35 tractor – the chassis of the M10 tank destroyer less the turret – towing an 8-inch gun in the Seventh Army sector.

2-The 978th of the Michigan National Guard formed on 8 Feb 43 from the 1st Bn, 119th FA, the 976th and 977th coming on 1 Mar 44 from the 35th FA.
3-The 634th on 24 Feb 44 at Anzio with the 1st Bn, 77th FA, the 173d and 985th on 28 Nov and 30 Oct 43 with the 173d FA. The 173d Bn is one of the few battalions to retain its trucks.
4-The 633d on 5 Mar 44 at Mignano with the 2d Bn, 36th FA.
5-The 190th at Utah Beach and the 200th at Omaha Beach, both from the Pennsylvania National Guard and formed in England out of the 190th FA on 1 November 43.
6-The 981st formed out of the 2d Bn, 144th FA on 2 Feb 43, the 979th with the 2d Bn, 119th FA on 8 Feb 43 and the 561st on 9 Jul 43.
7-The 732d (Colored) with trucks, activated at Fort Bragg on 21 Jan 43 and the 993d (Colored) with tractors, formed in Louisiana out of the 2d Bn, 353d FA on 1 Apr 43.

FIELD ARTILLERY BATTALIONS
(155 MM GUN)

Its first combat took place in Tunisia in March 1943, alongside battalions equipped with the 155 GPF. It seems that one single battery took part in the campaign, and that it was attached to the 34th Battalion, the 155 mm Howitzer M1 unit of the 9th Infantry Division.

It was not until the Sicilian operation that the 155 Gun appeared in battalion strength. On 30 August 1943, for example, four batteries apparently belonging to the 2d Battalion of the 36th FA Regiment attached to the 3d Infantry Division supported the attack by the 30th Infantry Regiment at Brolo, on the southern coast of the Island,

Then three battalions8, which had transited via North Africa, joined the Fifth Army in Italy on 10 October, three days before the crossing of the Volturno. They were next to being found on 15 August 1944 in Southern France, where they landed with a fourth battalion2 activated at the beginning of 1944. Two other similar battalions followed them and a third4 formed in the theater. The last to arrive would be the 530th Battalion, just one month before hostilities ended.

In the Southwest Pacific, the 223d Bn was already in action when it was formed in New Caledonia out of a battalion of the 200th Regiment. Released from the Americal Division in February 1943, it moved to the General Reserve and soon received its 155 mm guns, which it continued to tow with trucks. The 168th Bn of the Colorado National Guard only reached Australia in November 1943 and fought in New Guinea and the Philippines, as did the 983d originating from the same State, who went directly to the Philippines in May 1944. The 531st and 532d Bns followed to Saipan in June and the 226th of the New York National Guard, the 517th and the 433d landed in the Philippines between October 1944 and August 1945.

It was in Northwestern Europe where the majority of the 155 mm gun units – 34 Battalions – would be committed.

Formed in February 1943 out of the 1st Bn, 144th FA, the 980th landed on Utah Beach on D-Day. It was followed the next day by the 190th and the 200th5, then on 13 June by the 981st, on 27 June by the 979th and finally on 30 June by the 561st6.

Five battalions arrived in July, including the 559th, which had retained its tow trucks, and the 208th and 989th Bns formed from the 208th FA, a unit previously equipped with 155 mm GPF. Seven landed in August, including the four arriving from Italy with the Seventh Army and the 240th and 273d recently equipped in June, the former having exchanged its trucks for tractors and the latter its 105 mm howitzers for 155 mm guns. In October the 514th arrived, followed in December by the 516th and 261st which three months earlier had undergone the same transformation as the 240th and 273d.

Between January 18 and March 3 1945, nine additional battalions reached the Continent, including two formed at Fort Jackson, South Carolina in May 1944 out of elements of the 252d Coast Artillery Regiment. Finally, four battalions initially equipped with 155 mm guns and trucks or tractors, exchanged them at the close of 1944 against 8-inch howitzers. These included the 535th, 536th and 527th formed out of the 250th Coast Artillery Regiment.

In addition, two battalions[7] remaining in the United States were transformed into combat engineer battalions in March and May 1944.

Right from its first action in Tunisia, the "Long Tom" was a great success due to its long-range accuracy. In Italy the majority of rounds fired - 90% instead of the 20% allowed for in the regulations – used the maximum charge in order to be most effective in counter-battery work. And in Normandy, when the Third Army went over to the offensive, either one or two battalions of 155 Guns reinforced each attacking division.

FIELD ARTILLERY BATTALIONS
(155 MM GUN) (SELF-PROPELLED)

In a similar manner to the M7 howitzer, a 155 GPF Gun M1918A1 was mounted on the chassis of the M3 medium tank and adopted in March 1942 under the designation 155 mm Gun Motor Carriage M12, along with the Cargo Carrier M30. Then 100 units were built between September 1942 and March 1943.

From its first appearance, a great deal of publicity surrounded the most powerful self-propelled field gun in service. The American public was greatly impressed by the machine, to which the US Army public relations services had given the inappropriate nickname of "King Kong".

Distinctive unit insignia of the 174th FA Battalion formed in 1943, which arrived in France on 1 July 1944 with its S-P 155 mm guns. (Private Collection)

155 MM GUN MOTOR, CARRIAGE M12

The specifications of the M12 - also known as the 155 mm Gun M1918M1, Mount M3- are as follows:

- Manufacturer — GMC
- Weight in traveling order — 55,116 pounds
- Overall length — 21.4 ft
- Height — 8.7 ft
- Width — 8.13 ft
- Traverse — 28°
- Elevation — -5° to +30°
- Average rate of fire — 3 rounds/minute
- Sustained rate of fire — 1 round/minute
- Maximum range — 19,795 yards
- Practical range — 17,913 yards
- Road speed — 22 miles per hour
- Time for positioning — 15 minutes

A retractable spade anchored the unit to the ground and ensured stability when firing. The gun crew was composed of six men for the M12 (driver, chief of piece section, corporal and three gunners) and six for the M30 (driver, corporal in charge of the ammunition, and four gunners).

However, the Field Artillery was not interested, since it appeared badly adapted to a support function at corps level because of its limited elevation, and the majority of the machines were stored in a depot. On the other hand, the officers serving in Europe saw it as the ideal weapon to crush bunkers once the attack went in against the Siegfried Line. That was the reason why in February 1944, 75 mountings were fitted onto the newer Sherman M4 tank chassis for issue to six armored battalions intended for the European theater:

— the 258th and 991st formed in February 1943 out of the 258th Regiment (155 mm Gun) (Motorized) of the New York State National Guard

— the 174th and 987th formed at the same time in Texas out of the 174th Regiment (155 mm Gun) (Motorized)

— the 557th and the 558th activated in May 1943 in Oklahoma and California.

The first four arrived in England in January 1944 and went into action in France in July; the two others followed in August. Straightaway, the M12 proved itself to be an excellent gun that no bunker or tank could resist. But it was during the pursuit following the breakthrough at Avranches that its motor and its tracks – 200 miles (320 km) on the road were covered in the course of one day – and its old gun barrels performed so well, that the First Army was to recommend that a

battalion of M12s should be attached to each armored division.

In 1943-44 a parallel development resulted in the T83, made up of the chassis of the M4A3 tank mounting a 155 mm Gun M1A1. Put into production in February 1945, most arrived too late to take part in combat. But two prototypes were in fact sent to Germany for use by the New Equipment Study Mission. In this role they joined in the final operations alongside the M12s of the 991st Battalion.

FIELD ARTILLERY BATTALIONS (8-INCH HOWITZER)

As compared to the 155 mm gun, the development of its "twin" 8-inch howitzer (203 mm) was accelerated because the US Army had an urgent requirement for a piece of that caliber. Starting in 1928, the design finished as the 8-inch Howitzer T3, very advanced for its day and mounted on a carriage with pneumatic tires designed for truck haulage. It was this mounting which would later be used for the 155 mm gun.

However, no production examples would arrive prior to 1939. The T3 was approved late in the day in 1940 under

8-INCH HOWITZER M1, CARRIAGE M1

SPECIFICATIONS

• Weight in traveling order	31,970 pounds
• Overall length	36.75 ft
• Length of the barrel	16.9 ft
• Height	8.3 ft
• Width of the wheeled carriage	9.2 ft
• Weight of the wheeled carriage	5,380 pounds
• Tires	11.00x20
• Traverse	60°
• Elevation	1155 mils
• Max recoil at 0°	5 ft approx
• Max recoil at 63°	3 ft approx
• Average rate of fire	1 round/minute
• Sustained rate of fire	1 round every 2 minutes
• Maximum range	18,480 yards
• Muzzle velocity	1,950 ft/sec

• Time for positioning 1 to 6 hours

the designation M1, but production did not get underway until July 1942, due to a lack of funds. Most of its components were identical to those of the 155 mm gun, except for the recoil brake system which had to absorb the increased weight and recoil forces of the larger caliber weapon.

Normally designed for employment alongside the 240 mm howitzer, with which it shared the same breech, the mounting M1 and tractor, its primary role would be to join the corps artilleries and counter the German 17 cm K18.

Out of the 58 battalions formed on the howitzer, 46 were deployed overseas.

Three battalions formed in February 1943 arrived in Italy in the middle of November:
— the 194th and the 995th formed from the 194th Regiment whose 1st Battalion had received the first howitzers at Fort Bragg
— the 932d formed from the 1st Battalion of the 137th.

Then following the deactivation of the 17th Regiment, at Viticuso on 14 February 1944 its 2d Battalion took on the designation of 630th Bn equipped with the 8-inch Howitzer.

During the offensive in May, the 194th was inside the Anzio beachhead with VI Corps. The other battalions were in the Garigliano sector: the 932d with II Corps, the 630th and the 995th with the French Expeditionary Corps. Then the four battalions arrived in France: the 630th and the 995th on 9 September, the 932d on 20 November and the 194th on 22 November.

Accordingly, for three months the Fifth Army possessed no 8-inch howitzer unit, until the 527th and 534th Bns arrived on 1 March 1945. They had been formed in May 1944 and had exchanged their 155s six months before arriving in Italy.

The 8-inch Howitzer M1 – which had demonstrated its accuracy and the effectiveness of its projectiles compared to those dropped by the bomber squadrons, especially during the battles around Cassino – was thereafter widely deployed on the battlefields of Western Europe following the Normandy landings.

The 195th[8] was the first to arrive on 16 June 1944, followed on 26 June by the 793d[9] and the following day by the 997th[10]. Then on 17 July, the 578th and 999th[11] arrived from England.

In August, four battalions activated in June 1943 reached France, then three more in September, including the 207th Bn of the Oklahoma National Guard formed in the Canal Zone on 11 February 1942 out of the 2d Batta-

(National Archives)

lion, 158th FA and equipped with 105 mm Howitzers M2 up until taking ship at New York in July 1944.

Next, it was not until 1 January 1945 that the 535th arrived, having exchanged its 155 mm Guns just a few months earlier. Two other battalions followed at the close of January, then nine more in February and again a further nine in March. Out of these latter units, mostly activated in April of the previous year, twelve would stay in England for up to three months before moving to the Continent. No written record has come to light to explain whether this delay was

In Belgium on 28 December 1944, gunners of a 155 mm howitzer battalion assigned to the First Army are celebrating the coming of 1945 their own way. On the shell they are introducing in the breech, they have chalked up a message for the Fuehrer: "Happy New Year for Hitler".

Quadrant, Gunner's M1 (Mils) used to measure the elevation of the piece by placing the instrument on the reference surface of the barrel. (Artillery Museum, Draguignan

---

8-Attached to the 406th Group along with the 997th, it was formed at Fort Ord, California, on 1 Mar 43 from the 1st Bn, 195th Motorized Regiment.
9-Formed on these pieces at Fort Bragg, North Carolina, on 4 Mar 43.
10-Formed from the 2d Bn, 195th Regiment.
11-Formed from elements of the 578th FA (Colored) at Fort Bragg on 23 Feb 43.

HIGH SPEED TRACTOR M4 AND M5, ALLIS-CHALMERS

High Speed Tractor M4.
(colour plate by Nicolas Gohin)

TRACTOR HIGH SPEED, 18-ton M4

- Length — 203 inches
- Weight — 31 400 pounds
- Cruising range — 100 miles
- Speed — 21 mph
- Armament — 1 x .50 cal M2
- Crew — 10 men
- Ammunition carried — 30 rounds of 155 or 20 of 8-inch or 12 of 240

HIGH SPEED TRACTOR, 13-ton M5

- Length — 192 inches
- Weight — 28,275 pounds
- Cruisng range — 150 miles
- Speed — 30 mph
- Armament — 1 x .50 cal M2
- Crew — 9 men
- Ammunition carried — 24 rounds of 155 or 56 rounds of 105

High Speed Tractor M5.
(colour plate by Nicolas Gohin)

Distinctive unit insignia of the 35th FA Regiment (155 mm Gun) (Motorized) activated in February 1941. Having become a Group in March 1943, it was deployed to Italy the following November. (Le Poilu, Paris)

12- They were the 155 mm GMC M40 developed from the prototype T83 (394 built from February 1945) and the 8-inch HMC M43 developed from the T89 and adopted in July 1943 (48 built, from March 1945).

due to a lack of transport or the need for additional training.

In the Pacific, only seven battalions of 8-inch howitzers saw action. The first, the 465th Bn activated in March 1943 at Fort Bragg, exchanged its 75 mm pack howitzers for the 8-inch model on 15 January 1944, seven months before taking ship for New Guinea, from where it moved to the Philippines in October. The 655th followed it direct in January 1945, then the 749th and 750th landed on Okinawa with the first assault waves of the Tenth Army, while the 786th, 789th and 797th reached the Philippines between 9 and 11 July.

The most surprising aspect was the large number of battalions, which never left the United States, probably due to changing ideas on the use of heavy artillery. Five of them remained as 8-inch battalions up until the end of the war, but a further six underwent transformations and left the Artillery. The 795th (Colored) (Trk-D), formed in May 1943 at Fort Bragg, was transformed into a combat engineer battalion in March 1945. And at the beginning of July five other battalions formed in August and September of 1944 became chemical mortar battalions. Finally, the 576th Bn (8-inch S-P Howitzer) was activated on 16 October 1944 at Fort Bragg, with a provisional T/O&E drawn up on the basis of an experimental self-propelled heavy

artillery unit. This concept was of great interest to the Armor at the time, because of the extended mobility given to the pieces which enhanced their overall effectiveness. However, due to priorities elsewhere, the development and production of the S-P pieces had been significantly delayed. Two[12] were based on the modified chassis of the M4 medium tank with HVSS suspension, and two on the modified chassis of the M24 Chaffee light tank. However, apart from the two prototypes tried out in Germany – as noted above – none of this new equipment reached the combat units before the war ended.

FIELD ARTILLERY BATTALIONS (240 MM HOWITZER)

Having studied the French 240 mm howitzer and the American 7-inch naval gun adopted in 1917 and 1918, the Westervelt Board felt that in the future it would be desirable to be able to deploy similar types of weapon, suitably modernized. Preliminary studies were conducted during the 1920s and 1930s, but no prototype was in fact built since it was felt impossible to make them sufficiently mobile to keep pace with a motorized army. Nonetheless, thanks to the support of the Field Artillery Board, in 1940 the Ordnance Department re-launched the project to build the two super-heavy pieces which were adopted in 1942 as the 8-inch Gun M1 and the 240 mm Howitzer M1. Each one was transported on two special wagons: the barrel assembly and cradle on the first and the rest of the mounting on the second. A crane was required to assemble them at the firing point, and a special tractor was necessary to haul them. Despite this, the AGF seriously doubted that these enormous units would possess adequate cross-country mobility, and the US Army was loath to adopt them.

This was one of the reasons why neither super heavy piece was employed in North Africa in 1943. However, because the Germans had themselves made good use of similar pieces, it was finally decided to revise the requirement and upgrade their production priority, and to transform the chassis of superseded tanks into gun tractors. And so it was that several months later, even though the 155 mm gun had been judged adequate and that General Lucas, when commanding VI Corps, had cast doubt on the value of the 240 mm in Italy, it was decided to deploy them

in that theater. One of the reasons for the delay in the program was the existence in 1940 of 140 examples out of the 330 original 240 mm M1918 guns, based on a French design and manufactured under license in 1918-1919. Firing trials undertaken in 1924 had shown up several intractable problems, pointing to the need for a modernized version. In the end, 48 examples of the M1918 M1A1 were delivered to the Army to be used for training and Coast Defense, before they were declared obsolete in 1944.

A new program was launched in April 1944, and initial trails concentrated on producing a piece to be broken down for transport but which would be simple to assemble and position. Two three-axle carriages were finally chosen and the 240 mm Howitzer M1 on Carriage M1 was standardized in May 1943, although in fact the weapon had been in production since November of the previous year.

The 697th and the 698th, activated at Fort Bragg on 23 February 1943, reached Naples by way of North Africa on 22 and 24 January respectively, to take part in the battle around Cassino. Attached to II Corps, they joined combat in February and their five pieces fired a total of 900 shells each day. Then, during the

SPECIFICATIONS

• Weight of the barrel	25,122 pounds
• Weight of the mounting	39,635 pounds
• Total weight in firing order	64,756 pounds
• Length of the barrel	27.6 ft
• Traverse	400 mils
• One turn of the traversing handwheel	15 mils
• Elevation	1424 mils (15° to 65°)
• One turn of the elevating hand wheel	8 mils
• Average rate of fire	1 round every 2 minutes
• Sustained rate of fire	1 round every 4 minutes
• Range (maximum charge)	24,990 yards
• Range (heavy charge)	12,140 yards
• Range (light charge)	9,077 yards
• Muzzle velocity with maximum charge	2,300 ft/sec
• Time for positioning	One to two hours
• Weight of wagon M3 with accessories	15,212 pounds
• Overall length M3	41.7 ft
• Overall width M3	9.2 ft
• Height M3 loaded	10.8 ft
• Minimum turning radius	38 ft
• Tires	35.56x24
• Weight of wagon M2 with accessories	44,092 pounds
• Overall length M2 unloaded	27.2 ft
• Overall length M2 loaded	36.4 ft
• Overall width M2 unloaded	9.2 ft
• Height M2 loaded	6.9 ft
• Minimum turning radius	30 ft

240 mm HOWITZER M1, CARRIAGE M1

The 240 mm howitzer was transported on two wagons with pneumatic tires: the M2A1 for the barrel and the M3 for the mounting, towed by a HST M6. Assembly into firing configuration or disassembly into road configuration was by Mobile Crane M2.

(© National Archives)

On 20 August 1944, near Mantes-Gassicourt, an 8-in howitzer from the 999th FA Bn (Colored) is being put in position helped by its M4HST Tractor. This group and the 587th Battalion, which had arrived on French soil three days earlier, were the only two heavy artillery units made up of Afro-Americans.

Coast Artillery units
— the 543d and 545th activated in January and April 1944 respectively, having spent the intervening period in Hawaii.

TRACTOR HIGH SPEED, 18-ton M6	
• Length	260 inches
• Weight	76 000 pounds
• Cruisng range	125 miles
• Speed	15 mph
• Armament	1 x .50 cal M2
• Crew	10 men

Above:
At the end of autumn 1944, in Europe, an 8-in canon – barrel and recoil mechanism on a special trailer – is being moved, drawn by a tracked M35 Tractor derived from the tank destroyer chassis.

Above right.
High Speed Tractor M6.
(colour plate by Nicolas Gohin)

13- The third battery was inside the Anzio beachhead with VI Corps. During this period, Battery C was notable for its part in disabling the German armored train and railway gun nicknamed "Anzio Annie".
14-According to Shelby L. Stanton in Order of Battle, US Army, World War Two. Steven J. Zaloga in US Field Artillery of World War II does not give the number of the battalion but indicates that it underwent training in Hawaii and then in New Caledonia.
15-Up to 12 Aug 44, it lost two guns.

May offensive, the 697th supported II Corps on the left flank of the assault, and two batteries of the 698th[13] attached to the 194th Group supported the French Expeditionary Corps. The two battalions took an active and highly successful part in counter-battery and harassing fire on the rear sectors of the front and then, at the close of October, since the Italian theater had a lower priority, they moved to France.

The 551st, 552d and 553d, activated in August 1943, fought there from early July 1944. Eight other battalions that had exchanged their 105 mm Howitzers M2 for 240s followed them: landing between 4 July and 2 September, they were divided up between the various corps. Then on 3 April 1945 two battalions arrived which had been formed in the previous August with the gunners of two battalions of Coast Artillery.

Elsewhere, from May 1943 onward, tests were undertaken with a pair of tracked mountings, the M3 and M2 Carriages having caused problems moving on soft ground. Two units were proved to be satisfactory, (the T16E1 for the barrel assembly and the T17E1 for the mounting), so in June 1944 the AGF authorized the production of six howitzers of the modified type to equip a battalion destined for deployment in the Pacific. Accordingly, the 544th, activated on 12 January 1944, went into combat in New Guinea in mid-November 20 and arrived on Luzon on February 19 1945, just in time to take part in the operation to liberate Manila.

It would in fact be the only unit with the new model to go into action, the six others at Fort Bragg only reaching the Philippines in July 1945:
— the 778th and 779th activated in May 1944 from two

And at the same time, the 560th remained at Fort Bragg and was transformed into a chemical mortar battalion

FIELD ARTILLERY BATTALIONS (8-INCH GUN)

Activated as a 105 mm battalion in November 1942 at Fort Bliss, Texas, the 153d left the 1st Cavalry Division in March 1943 before the latter's departure for California. Subsequently equipped with the 8-inch gun, it reached England in March 1944 and landed in France on 26 June. Seven days later, it went into action for the first time. The three following battalions, which arrived between 7 and 27 August, were also former 105 mm

units, having exchanged their equipment shortly before taking ship for Europe.

The 575th was activated on 20 July[14] 1944 at Terricciola with one single firing battery. While it waited to take part in the Dragoon operation with the Seventh Army, its 3d Battery was attached to the 697th Bn armed with the 240 mm howitzer as part of IV Corps[15]. The battalion reached France in August and on 18 November the other two batteries were activated.

In the Pacific theater, two battalions activated in April 1944 and a third formed out of a Coast Artillery unit, arrived in the Philippines on 3 August 1945 when the last Japanese troops had ceased fighting on Mindanao Island.

8-INCH GUN M1, CARRIAGE M2

Designed at the same time as the 240 mm Howitzer, the 8-inch Gun shared many common features: the same breech assembly, car-

riages, mountings and haulage vehicles. The problem of the latter was solved by using the chassis of the obsolescent M3 Grant tank or of the M10 Tank Destroyer held in the storage depots. The minor differences were limited to those changes necessary to take into account the weight of the barrel and the recoil forces.

The production of these two super-heavy pieces was as follows:

	1942	1943	1944	1945	Total
8-inch Gun M1	10	49	57	23	139
240 mm Howitzer M16		57	158	94	315

SPECIFICATIONS
- Barrel assembly weight   30,005 pounds
- Total weight in firing position 79,366 pounds
- Barrel length   34.1 ft
- Traverse   40°
- Elevation   10° to 50°
- Average rate of fire   2 rounds/minute
- Sustained rate of fire   1 round every 2 minutes
  - Maximum range   35,105 yards
  - Normal range   29,856 yards
  - Minimum range   10,794 yards
  - Muzzle velocity with max. charge   2,838 ft/sec
  - Time for positioning from one to two hours.

THE "AUXILIARY" ARTILLERY

*An M4 Sherman
of the 752d Tank Battalion
fitted with the Rocket
Launcher M17,
with twenty 7.2-inch
rockets, seen during
the closing days
of the war in Italy.*

1-T/O 6-85 dated 10 Apr 45, with 41
GMC trucks, 75 Dodges and 29 Jeeps.
2-The battalion had a total of 29 Jeeps,
35 Dodge 4x4s, 40 Dodge 6x6s and
41 GMC trucks.

GIVEN THAT the rocket launcher battalions only appeared towards the close of the war and in an almost anecdotal fashion, all throughout the conflict units with specific armament, which did not belong to the Field Artillery, were nevertheless employed in fire support:

— either because that was their specific role, such as the chemical mortars belonging to the Chemical Warfare Service, and the cannon companies manned by the Infantry
— or else because their equipment – tank destroyers, tanks,

antiaircraft guns – lent themselves to this role. These units and their weapons constitute what is sometimes referred to as the "auxiliary" artillery.

ROCKET FIELD ARTILLERY BATTALIONS
(4.5-inch & 7.2-inch rockets)

For many years, the Field Artillery gunners showed little interest in rockets. It was not until 1943 that a reluctant the US Army, spurred into action by the examples of other belligerent powers, drew up a list of specific requirements.

Several mountings for the self-contained 4.5-inch (112.5 mm) rocket were tested and some went into service:

— T27 with eight rockets, ground mounted or mounted in a

(National Archives)

*Shoulder patch
of the 83d Chemical
Battalion (Motorized).
(Private Collection*

double row on the back of a GMC truck, used in Europe towards the close of 1944

— T34 with 60 rockets, mounted on the turret of a Sherman, used in Italy and in Western Europe in 1944 and 1945

— T44 with 108 tubes installed in the hull of the DUKW amphibious truck, with 250 examples produced, used in the Pacific

— T45 with 14 naval rockets mounted in a double row on a Jeep and later a DUKW, with 2,000 examples produced, used in the Pacific from 1944 onward

— T66 Honeycomb with 24 rockets mounted on wheels, with 500 examples produced, used experimentally in Czechoslovakia and later in the Pacific.

Performance was poor: the M8 rocket with a range of 4,160 yards (3,800 m) and the M16 reaching 5,250 yards (4,800 m) had barely the effectiveness of a 105 shell on arrival at the target.

The naval 7.2-inch (18 cm) rocket with a maximum range of 3,280 yards (3,000 m) and about the same effect on target was adopted on two mountings:

— T32 Xylophone with four rows of eight projectiles mounted on the flat bed of a GMC

— T40 (or M17) with 20 projectiles mounted on a Sherman, 580 examples produces, used in the Pacific from June 1945 onward and the only type to be retained post-war.

The 12th FA Battalion of the 2d Infantry Division, with disappointing results, tested the multiple rocket launcher T27 in August 1944 during the siege of Brest. Next, the 94th Division used large numbers in September and October in the Lorient sector. 75 examples of the T32 were then delivered to the 18th FA Bn equipped with the 105 mm Howitzer M2, who used them in November facing the Siegfried Line and during the battle of the Ardennes. But then their use became less frequent, and they fell from favor, due to the wide dispersal of the rockets, their relatively poor range, and the fact that the Germans were accustomed to react rapidly and effectively.

In the Pacific, two battalions equipped solely with the T34 mounting were deployed prior to the end of the war. They were the 421st and 422d activated at Fort Sill on 12 April 1945 from the 1st and 2d Rocket Battalions set up on 4 January, previously equipped as two antiaircraft units. The former reached Hawaii on 12 June and was committed on Okinawa on 24 July, while the latter went directly to the Philippines, arriving on 11 July.

Four other battalions, armed with the T66, were set up during 1945, but too late to take part in combat operations:

— three at Fort Sill after handing over their 105 Howitzers, having come from the Replacement and School Command

— one at Camp Polk, Louisiana, handing in their 8-inch Howitzers.

Each battalion was composed of 34 officers and 645 enlisted men[1] split between a headquarters & headquarters battery, three firing batteries and one service battery. The firing battery had two sections with six T66 mounts, for a total of 288 launch tubes, able to engage a range of targets. The mounting consisted of a trailer carrying 24 launch tubes and weighing 1,213 pounds (550 kg) – as against 4,189 pounds (1,900 kg) for the 105 mm Howitzer M2, and was normally hauled by a Dodge 6x6. The squad for one mounting was made up of the chief and four gunners, of whom one would be the aimer. The rate of fire was one salvo every 24 seconds.

The transport capacity of the battalion was 5,328 rounds, of which 2,880 were carried in the 21/2-ton trucks and 1-ton trailers of the service battery[2]. It was recognized that a battalion of 894 launch tubes could neutralize the same surface area as three battalions of 105s.

By the end of the war, the American gunners were of the opinion that in no way could the rockets replace classic field artillery. The only possible use would be for zone neutralization, excluding any firing at targets of limited size or sited too close to friendly troops. All considered, the rapid rate of fire and the maneuverability of the mountings in no way compensated for their poor range and lack of accuracy.

CHEMICAL BATTALIONS (MOTORIZED)

In 1924, the Chemical Warfare Service tested a 4.2-inch mortar (106 mm), developed from the British 4-inch version used in the Great War. But since the War Department favored the 81 mm mortar for deploying poison gas or laying down smoke screens, the project was abandoned. However, the heavy mortar had several advantages: it was capable of laying down significant firepower in a short time, and thanks to its high angle capability it could hit targets in defile that other weapons could not. In addition, its short range and its mobility made it suitable for infantry support.

That was why in 1934 the CWS began trials with high explosive shells, even though their primary mission was the delivery of chemical ordnance, and two years later they adopted the 4.2-inch Chemical Mortar M1A1. Later, in 1941, when clearly there was a requirement for a short-range infantry support weapon, the CWS undertook the specific production of a standardized HE mortar shell, and asked that the firing of such missiles be recognized as a primary mission for the chemical mortar units. Although the Services of Supply were in agreement, the Army Ground Forces were opposed. Moreover, the latter countered with the proposal that, following trials by the Field Artillery Board, the Field Artillery should take control of these mortars in order to employ them in theaters of operations which lacked 105 mm howitzers.

Finally, after lengthy discussions, in March 1943 the WD authorized the use of high explosive mortar shells and changes to the regulations to suit this new doctrine. However, they specified that the battalions should be integrated into the Artillery fire control and signals network. In the meantime, development had continued, and the M2 model mortar, incorporating a more robust base plate and barrel in order to fire heavier shells a greater distance, was adopted.

Weighing in at only 300 pounds (135 kg), the weapon ranged out initially to 3,170 yards (2,900 m). The rate of fire varied between five and twenty rounds a minute, and it took five minutes in daylight and ten minutes at night to position the mortar. There were two types of HE ammunition:

— the M3 HE & Incendiary shell, weighing 24.25 pounds (11 kg)

— the M4 shell weighing 35.25 pounds (16 kg), with a short range of only 985 yards (900 m).

After war was declared, the battalion became the standard

*4.2-in mortar transport cart photographed
next to the Jeep's 1/4 ton trailer
for comparison.*

Barrels and ammunition for a company of "chemical" mortars, carried on the backs of mules in Italy.

Collar badge of the Chemical Warfare Service. (Private Collection)

3-T/O 3-25, Chemical Motorized Battalion (Separate) dated 1 Apr 42.
4-The 3d Battalion in particular was attached to the French Expeditionary Corps. On 12 Jan 45, a shell fell on a company CP where the battalion commander and five of his officers were meeting: all were killed.

mortar unit. Therefore in January 1942 two chemical battalions (motorized) were activated:

— the 2d, formed from elements stationed at Edgewood Arsenal in Maryland since 1935

— the 3d Bn activated at Fort Benning, Georgia.

Next, four others – the 81st, 82d, 83d and 84th – were activated in April and June, and GHQ planned to form six more by year end, followed by twelve in 1943 and a further twelve in 1944. Then in 1943 when the decision was taken to send the "chemical" mortars into action in Sicily, the WD authorized the activation of four additional units: the 86th, 87th, 88th and 85th.

A battalion had a strength of 1,010 men, including 36 officers, divided between a headquarters and headquarters company and four weapons companies[3] with two platoons of two squads of three mortars, 48 in total for the battalion, plus 124 vehicles of which 88 were GMC trucks.

The four battalions that reached North Africa between January and April 1943 took no part in the Tunisian campaign. However, they went into action during the invasion of Sicily, the 2d, 3d and 83d being each attached to an assault division with the 84th being held in reserve. Despite having received little training in amphibious operations or alongside infantrymen or the tankers, neither of whom understood the characteristics of this new weapon, the chemical battalions performed well. They carried out a large number of accurate preparation, interdiction or neutralization barrages with HE shells. The reaction from commanders in the field was rather favorable, most recommending that every infantry division should be supported by the mortars.

However, their means of transportation were not well suited: the GMC trucks were highly visible on the mortar positions and the inadequate handcarts planned for use on difficult terrain would have to be replaced by Jeeps borrowed from the Infantry or by pack mules. One other problem was their limited range. In fact the units fighting in Sicily had not yet been issued with the new ammunition which would have given their mortars greater reach thanks to the use of new propellants – 3,500 yards (3,200 m) by January 1943 and even up to 4,375 yards (4,000 m) by the following May. Even worse, the CWS had decided to lay down 3,170 yards (2,900 m) as the maximum practical range, but they relented on this decision in May, at the request of the Seventh Army and the theater commanders. But this about-face occurred only progressively, although by December all the battalions in Italy had received new ammunition extending the range of their mortars to 4,800 yards (4,400 m).

CHEMICAL MORTAR BATTALIONS

The 2d, 83d and 84th Battalions next landed at Salerno on 10 September 1943 and for four days took part in the defense of the beachhead which was threatened by German counterattacks. Joined in October by the 3d Battalion, the four fought as part of the Fifth Army: the 84th up until the end of the war, the three others up until July 1944[4]. Then to make up for those units which had left for France, two battalions were formed in August out of the elements of two antiaircraft battalions which had been inactivated in Oran the previous month: the 99th at Caserta and the 100th in the Naples region.

In Italy, where the fighting was bitter, the 4.2-inch mortar crews worked miracles, and the infantry commanders who had at first been skeptical of their abilities, changed their minds after having seen them in action. In fact they wanted the mortars to remain

Shoulder patch of the 2d Chemical Mortar Battalion, which went in with the first waves in two landings: in Sicily in July 1943 and in Southern France in August 1944. It represents a dragon spitting lightning, on a blue and gold background. (Le Poilu, Paris)

in full-time support of their infantry. The three battalions withdrawn from Italy next landed in Southern France with the Seventh Army[5] and were joined in December by the 99th Battalion.

Well trained in amphibious operations, the 81st and the 87th Battalions landed in Normandy on 6 June 1944. On 27 June the 92d Bn formed in England in February joined them, then on 29 June by the 86th Bn. During the advance as far as Metz, there was less call on the battalions due to a lack of determined resis-

tance on the part of the enemy. Then eight other battalions arrived in France, either directly from the States or by way of England. They had been formed between November 1943 and May 1944: the 91st arrived in October, the 93d and 95th in January 1945, the 89th, 90th and 97th in February, and finally the 94th and 96th in March.

As per the plan set in September 1943 and put into effect in June 1944, the total manpower of each battalion reduced from

A 4.2-inch Mortar of the 87th Chemical battalion in action in an orchard in Normandy, in July 1944. Activated in May 1943 at Camp Rucker, Alabama, the Battalion took ship for England one year later.

Opposite, left: 4.2-in mortar section being trained in the United States.

5-Two companies carried in gliders joined in the airborne operation: Company A of the 2d Bn with the British 2d Parachute Brigade and Company D of the 83d Bn with the 517th Parachute Infantry Regiment.

(National Archives)

1,010 to 622. Then because the shortfall in manpower continued to bite, it was decided to suppress the fourth company in the battalions stationed in France and in Italy. The theoretical establishment was however then slightly increased to 672 officers and enlisted men. Nine Dodge 6x6 were added to the vehicle park, and the three companies were subdivided into three sections of four mortars each. Finally the new organization – only coming into effect in a progressive manner between December 1944 and April 1945 – was marked by the adoption of the designation "Chemical Mortar Battalion", probably because it was no longer necessary to keep their role a secret.

As for employment, the controversy over tactical control continued to be a problem: the CWS was in favor of those who felt that control should lie with the Infantry units being supported, while others – including former artillerymen – felt that control should revert to the Artillery.

The 82d Battalion was first deployed in New Caledonia from July 1943. Then, prior to the offensive in New Guinea, unable to wait for the arrival of the units which had been detailed to join

his forces, General MacArthur obtained approval to transform the 641st Tank Destroyer Battalion. At the close of the operation, on June 24 1944 this unit was officially redesignated the 98th Chemical Battalion.

With the Sixth Army at Leyte were the 85th, 88th and 89th. They were followed to the Philippines in February 1945 by the 80th which had been activated in June 1944. Finally, activated in December 1944, the 71st took part in combat operations on Okinawa in August 1945, while the 72d remained in Hawaii.

Nine independent companies also operated in the Pacific, among them the 91st, formed in Hawaii in March 1942 from one company of the disbanded 1st Battalion, and the 189th Chemical Mortar Company (Separate) formed in July 1944. One of the other special features of the operations in the Pacific was the use of mortars embarked on landing craft[6]. Lastly, seven battalions were established rather late in the day in June 1945 out of seven heavy artillery battalions being formed in the United States.

More than 6,000 mortars were produced during the war for

6-Landing Craft, Infantry (Mortar) #739 to #742 were thus armed by the men of the 88th and 91st and by infantrymen of the 111th Regiment.

7-In the advance on Metz, for example, the 81st Bn fired more than 30,000 shells.

the Army and the Marine Corps. Such large numbers were needed for replacement purposes, because the mortars saw intensive use at maximum charge[7].

INFANTRY CANNON COMPANIES

In 1941 when the creation of an airborne division was being considered, it was planned to equip it with 105 mm howitzers carried in aircraft. As the 105 mm Howitzer M2 took up too much space, it was first decided to use a shortened version of its barrel on the M3A1 mounting of the 75 mm field gun. But during the trials it was found that the slow burning powder used in the normal rounds would not work: the flame and blast at the muzzle were too fierce and the propellant did not burn completely. Apart from this problem with the ammunition – which was resolved by modifying the original round - the results were satisfactory and the piece was adopted under the designation 105 mm Howitzer M3 on Mounting M3, or M3A1 with a stronger trail assembly. However, since production only started in 1943, the airborne battalions – as noted earlier – were equipped with the 75 mm Pack Howitzer M8.

The same development could be observed in the infantry cannon companies. On 1 April 1942, as part of the conversion to the triangular structure, each infantry regiment received a cannon company. This development was the outcome of lengthy debates, and was meant to serve the needs of the Infantry who, just as in the previous conflict, had suffered because the Artillery could not move up as quickly as the infantrymen on foot.

Since no *ad hoc* equipment was available, the cannon companies had to be equipped with substitute howitzer motor carriages: the T30 for the 75 mm and the T19 for the 105, both using modified M3 half-tracks. Conforming to the initial table of organization[8], the cannon company of the motorized infantry regiment would therefore consist of two platoons of three 75s plus one platoon of two 105s, operated by 123 infantrymen. This was the arrangement in use when the three units of the 1st Infantry Division went into action in Tunisia and then Sicily.

Otherwise, various models of the pack howitzer were used: the M3 in Tunisia, the M8 in the Pacific and the M1 on pack mule, also in the Pacific, and in Burma and India. But the artillerymen looked unfavorably on this substitute equipment – and especially the self-propelled pieces – which encouraged the infantrymen to employ them for other roles, notably against tanks.

However, these moves were only temporary expedients and, despite the good results being achieved, the Army Ground Forces still wanted to provide a more powerful weapon for the parachute troops. At the same time, it posed the question of whether

105 MM HOWITZER M3, CARRIAGES M3 AND M3A1

A 105 mm Howitzer M3 at firing exercises in a training camp in the United States. Like the gunners, the crew is armed with the M1 Carbine.

The howitzer developed for the airborne artillery also suited the infantry "gunners" who received the largest numbers and in fact were served first. The supply of this equipment to the airborne divisions proceeded much more slowly: it had originally been planned to equip them with three battalions of 75s for direct support plus one battalion of 105s for general support. In the final resort, only the two glider-borne units (319th and 320th Battalions) of the 82d Airborne Division were equipped with the 105 mm Howitzer M3.

The howitzer was normally towed by a Dodge 6x6 in the infantry units and by a Jeep in the airborne artillery. 1,965 were produced in 1943, 410 in 1944 and 205 in 1945, for a total of 2,580[1] before production ceased.

1-Including the 64 supplied to the French for their infantry cannon companies initially activated with a cadre of artillery personnel.

SPECIFICATIONS

Weight in traveling order	2,490 pounds
Overall length	13.1 ft
Overall width	5.6 ft
Traverse	45°
Elevation	-9° to +30°
Rapid rate of fire	6 rounds per minute
Sustained rate of fire	2 rounds per minute
Time for positioning	1 minute
Maximum range	8,200 yards
Towing speed	25 miles per hour

Shoulder patch of the Tank Destroyer Forces approved in September 1942 and worn up until 1947. (Private Collection)

M10 Tank Destroyers take part in an artillery barrage prior to the assault of a village in the northern Apennines.

8- Four antitank battalions armed with the 37 mm and five battalions of 75 mm taken from various units.

	TD (S-P) Bn	TD (Towed) Bn
T/O	18-25	18-35
Strenght	671	797
Armored cars	36	14
Other vehicles	86	141

the cannon companies were essential, because of the fact that each infantry regiment would have an artillery battalion attached to it. Again, self-propelled pieces took up more shipping space, weighed a lot more, were very vulnerable in the field and consumed more fuel than a towed piece of ordnance. As a result, the cannon company was suppressed in the T/O of March 1943 and replaced by three sections of two 105 howitzers included in the regimental command company. Then in June 1943 the cannon company was re-established with three platoons of two 105 Howitzers M3 as and when these latter pieces were delivered. There were evidently a few exceptions to the rule, as certain units in the Pacific were equipped with S-P M7s.

TANK DESTROYERS

Although the Battle of France in 1940 had shown the importance of antitank warfare, the US Army had not succeeded in drawing up a coherent tactical doctrine. To start the ball rolling, in 1941 the head of the Operations and Training Division (G-3) of the GHQ brought together representatives from the various interested parties: the Infantry, Field Artillery, Armored Force, Cavalry, Coast Artillery, the GHQ and the Planning Division.

Even if all present wished for increased growth in antitank capability and the incorporation of appropriate battalions in the Divisions, they could not agree on which arm of service should have overall responsibility, as several put themselves forward: the Infantry who claimed to be the only party with the necessary experience, the Field Artillery who possessed the weapons best adapted for an antitank role, and the Cavalry which felt they possessed sufficient impetus to make it work. For its part, the GHQ wanted the antitank units to be grouped together into an independent antitank force, which would form part of the General Reserve. Finally, G-3 proposed that the Infantry should be responsible up until the official creation of the Armored Force, whereupon that Force would take charge, whether it wanted to or not.

Annoyed by these conflicting opinions which reminded him of the controversy which led up to the foundation of the original Armored Force, on 24 June 1941 General Marshall gave the order to create an antitank battalion inside each division. Then on 8 August General McNair ordered the Third Army to put together from its own resources[8] three provisional groups each consisting of three antitank battalions. Opposing the armored divisions during the maneuvers in Louisiana and the Carolinas, these groups had some success, and on 27 November the War Department decided to form 53 battalions under the designation of "Tank Destroyer", to better reflect "their offensive spirit". Then on 3 December, the divisional battalions were placed under the control of GHQ and all received a number in the following series which corresponded to their origins: 600 for the infantry division, 700 for the armored division and 800 for the eleven units from the Field Artillery. The tank destroyer had been born, but it lacked both tactical doctrine and suitable armament.

It had quickly become apparent that the 37 mm gun was inadequate for the task, so much so that in 1942 all the battalions were reformed as heavy S-P types, equipped with twenty four 75 mm guns mounted on the M3 half-track. However, the high silhouette and the mediocre antitank performance of these weapons in Tunisia caused a revision to a towed gun which would be easier to camouflage and protect. A test battalion equipped with 3-inch guns (76.2 mm) was therefore formed at Fort Hood, Texas in January 1943, and the S-P battalions still present in the United States were progressively converted to towed guns.

The decision was then taken in January 1944 to equip half the units with the Gun Motor Carriage M10 which had the same

75 MM HOWITZER MOTOR, CARRIAGE T30

Otherwise, various models of the pack howitzer were used: the M3 in Tunisia, the M8 in the Pacific and the M1 on pack mule, also in the Pacific, and in Burma and India. But the artillerymen looked unfavorably on this substitute equipment – and especially the self-propelled pieces – which encouraged the infantrymen to employ them for other roles, notably against tanks.

However, these moves were only temporary expedients and, despite the good results being achieved, the Army Ground Forces still wanted to provide a more powerful weapon for the parachute troops. At the same time, it posed the question of whether the cannon companies were essential, because of the fact that each infantry regiment would have an artillery battalion attached to it. Again, self-propelled pieces took up more shipping space, weighed a lot more, were very vulnerable in the field and consumed more fuel than a towed piece of ordnance. As a result, the cannon company was suppressed in the T/O of March 1943 and replaced by three sections of two 105 howitzers included in the regimental command company.

Then in June 1943 the cannon company was re-established with three platoons of two 105 Howitzers M3 as and when these latter pieces were delivered. There were evidently a few exceptions to the rule, as certain units in the Pacific were equipped with S-P M7s.

SPECIFICATIONS

Weight in traveling order	19,346 pounds
Overall length	19.7 ft
Height	7.9 ft
Armament	75 mm Howitzer M3 (modified)
Maximum range	9,460 yards
Traverse	50°
Elevation	-9° to +50°
Maximum road speed	44 miles per hour
Crew	5

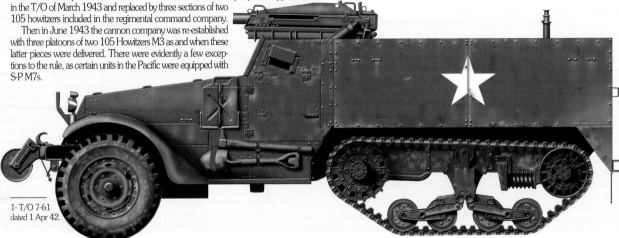

1- T/O 7-61
dated 1 Apr 42.

French Manual on Tank Destroyer gunfire, copied partly from the American version, in which Chapter III devoted to indirect firing takes up 43 pages out of the total of 61. (Private Collection)

5th August 1944. A M4A-1 76 mm and a Howitzer Motor Carriage M8 from the 3rd Armored Division, near Barenton.

chassis as the Sherman, was armed with the 3-inch Gun, and weighed 28 tons. The two different types of battalion thereafter differed as regards their strength, their armament, and the number of their vehicle.

With its 36 guns, the TD battalion was an important adjunct to the divisional artillery, as it doubled the division's firepower. That was the reason why artillery support became its secondary mission, and it was used on an increasingly frequent basis for harassing and interdiction fire alongside the DA.

But during the fighting in the Bocage of Normandy, the towed gun was found to be difficult to maneuver, while the S-P antitank gun was appreciated by the infantrymen for the immediate support it could bring to them. Then new machines armed with 76 mm and 90 mm guns began deliveries to the units, replacing the M10s and the towed guns.

For either type, their employment as artillery remained important. Their involvement was made easier by the specialized topographical equipment available in the European Theater, along with the established system of fire control, and also the presence in the TD units of ex-Field Artillery officers. However, experience showed that these units possessed neither sufficient quantities of telephone cable to maintain a signals network for prolonged periods, nor the topographical officers needed for work outside their positions. In addition, as their allocation of HE shells was limited, and self-propelled guns were in constant demand, and so the towed guns were those most often called upon, as much as they existed. Then in 1945, the relative absence of enemy armor led the S-P battalions to be frequently employed as close mobile artillery support.

TANK, ASSAULT GUNS
AND ANTIAIRCRAFT GUNS

The tank destroyer units were not the only ones to be used from 1943 onwards more and more as auxiliary field artillery. This was equally the case with the tanks and the antiaircraft guns.

This tendency first appeared in mid-1943 when Allied Force Headquarters in Algiers informed Washington that the commanders in the field wanted the TD battalions to improve their indirect fire capabilities. The AGF accepted the suggestion, but also included the tanks – for which no such request had been made –

	Weight in tons	Gun caliber in mm	Gun range in yards
M4A4 Sherman	30	75	13,300
M26 Pershing	41	90	13,000
M10A1	28.6	76.2	13,700
M18 Hellcat	17	76.2	13,700
M36 Jackson	27.7	90	12,800

as General McNair considered the latter in principal to be a specific form of artillery. A commission was therefore established, which immediately identified the problems cause by a lack of specialized equipment and the necessary training, and suggested that less ambitious targets should be set. At the same time, the AGF G-3 felt that the tanks should remain with the Armor and that the tank destroyer units should be assimilated into the Field Artillery.

The problem was the familiar one of having to find the proper balance between two solutions, each one with its own advantages and disadvantages. The directive sent out on 6 November by the AGF therefore sought to retain the advantages of multi-functioning without losing the advantages of specialization. Emphasis should be laid on the respective principal missions, and the secondary mission of reinforcing the artillery firepower could be utilized only when the primary mission was not called for, where no additional personnel were necessary, and when the fire support mission fell within the limitations of the specific equipment issued. Moreover, the fire coordination, target designation, telephone network and other equipment maintenance, would normally be the responsibility of the divisional and corps artilleries to which the independent tank and tank destroyer battalions would be attached for their fire support mission.

The details of the various armored vehicles available for such duties at the end of the war were as follows:

In addition, the assault guns of the armored units could carry out indirect fire missions when required. They were:

— three 105 mm Howitzer M4 in the separate tank battalions

— six S-P 105 mm Howitzers M7 in the armored infantry battalions

— six or eight Howitzer Motor Carriage M8 armed with a 75 mm in the reconnaissance squadrons or a battery of six S-P 105 mm Howitzers in certain independent units.

During the winter of 1943-44 in Italy, the aerial threat had diminished enough to allow the antiaircraft battalions to begin to join in ground fires, with the larger units to which they normally gave antiaircraft protection. Considered for the first time as auxiliary field artillery during the Cassino battle, when they were not engaged in firing at enemy aircraft the 90 mm AA guns were used in ground combat. Rapidly becoming famous under the name of "Baby Long Tom", they alone fired 40,000 rounds during the attack on the Gustav Line and the breakout from Anzio, harassing enemy artillery, neutralizing strong points and dispersing troop concentrations.

Officially, even if their secondary antitank role had long been acknowledged, the 90 mm units had to wait until April 1944 for the AGF and then the War Department to formally assign to them the role of auxiliary field artillery, with the same conditions as applied to the tanks and tank destroyers. Accordingly, two weeks of training and a month of service in the field spent in ground firing were added to the training program of each AA unit prior to their deployment overseas. That was the price to pay for the Field Artillery to benefit from the invaluable support from the 16 guns of each AAA gun battalion.

Elsewhere, the 155 mm gun mobile battalions formed for close defense of port areas were employed as classic heavy artillery on the Pacific islands.

(National Archives)

(National Archives)

TOWARDS A SINGLE ARTILLERY

During the months that followed the end of operations in the Pacific, the American field artillery – as with the whole of the Army – underwent a drastic reduction of its manpower and units. From 696 in December 1944, the number of battalions in service dropped to 310 twelve months later, in other words fewer than on the declaration of war.

The organization of units within the National Guard and the Organized Reserves did make 198 additional battalions available at the close of 1946, plus an extra 431 in 1947, which went some way towards compensating for the cuts in the Regular Army.

In fact, studies on the return of the forces in Europe back to the United States had begun in November 1944, as part of the redeployment to the Pacific theater. Overall, in March 1945 it was planned to retain a total of 53 of infantry, armor or airborne divisions. Then in June the War Department imposed a model of an infantry division containing 16,000 officers and men, or 3,000 less than the number envisaged by the AGF. The overall organization of the Field Artillery was not to be affected. Provision was even made to increase battalion strength by 320 gunners assigned to signals, to range mortar fire and to increase the number of pieces per battery from four to six. Elsewhere, the cannon companies exchanged their towed howitzers for self-propelled pieces.

The instruction passed to the European and Mediterranean theaters was therefore to reorganize their Divisions along the lines of the new table of organization, either prior to departing from Europe, or else within the United States with advance personnel sent from Europe. Then in July, less rigid plans were adopted, taking into account the operations still underway in the Pacific and the availability of personnel and equipment in the United States and in Europe.

At first, only two reassigned divisions – the 86th and the 97th – reached the Philippines in September 1945 out of the 66 repatriated between July 1945 and April 1946. During the same period, three were disbanded in Germany and eight in the Far East, so that by the end of that period only four were stationed in Germany, one in Italy and seven in Korea or Japan.

For the field artillery battalions, the repatriations followed by disbandment stretched over a period of eight months between September 1945 and April 1946, in no particular order but at a steady pace. 311 batta-

On 4 July 1945, American forces completed the occupation of their sector of Berlin. The 105 M7 self-propelled guns of the 2nd Armored Division fire a salvo in honour of Independence Day, celebrated in the capital of the vanquished Reich. The war in Europe is over, the post-war era is about to begin. But five years later the Korean War started.

lions were therefore inactivated with a peak of 60 in October rising to 80 in December. 44 were inactivated on site: 12 in Italy, 7 in France, 7 in Germany, 2 in Austria, 10 in the Philippines, 2 in Korea and 4 in Japan.

Meanwhile, beginning in the summer of 1945, a commission led by Lieutenant General Alexander M. Patch – who was the Seventh Army commander in Europe until June – met to examine the role and the missions of the various arms within the Army, and to make recommendations for its future organization bearing in mind the lessons learnt from the war, but also the possibilities of new technological advances.

As for the division, certain modifications only served to reinforce the facts. Therefore, the antiaircraft battalion that was systematically "attached" would henceforth become an integral part. But others were more innovative, especially as regards the Artillery. They were an increase from four to six of the number of pieces in field artillery batteries of a caliber up to and including 155 mm, and the union under a common command of the field and antiaircraft artilleries with, at a future date to be determined, the addition of the coast defense artillery.

In the new T/O published in 1947, the artillery of the infantry division retained its four battalions, but its towed howitzers were only retained on a provisional basis pending the arrival of sixteen new self-propelled versions per battalion which were then still in the design stage. It would receive a battalion of four firing batteries with self-propelled pieces and radar equipment to locate enemy artillery and mortar positions. As for the artillery of the armored division, it would receive a battalion of self-propelled 155 mm howitzers as well as an antiaircraft battalion.

For the arm branches, the Army Organization Act of 1950, which appeared on the eve of the Korean War, created one sole artillery made up of the field artillery joined together with the antiaircraft artillery ceded by the former Coast Artillery. The units were to retain their designations of Field Artillery (FA) or Antiaircraft Artillery (AAA) corresponding with their primary role.

ACKNOWLEDGEMENTS

The author is grateful for the assistance given by Lieutenant Colonel Gilles Aubagnac, Curator of the Musée de l'Artillerie in Draguignan,
Mrs. de Mirandol and Mr. Viguereux his assistants,
by the historical souvenir shop Le Poilu in Paris,
and by Mr. Philippe Charbonnier.

BIBLIOGRAPHY

George Forty. *US Army Handbook 1939-45,* Ian Allan Ltd, London 1979

Christofer R. Gabel. *The US Army GHQ Maneuvers of 1941,* US Army Center of Military History, Washington DC, 1991

Ken Roberts Greenfield, Robert R. Palmer, Bell I. Wiley. *The Organization of Ground Combat Troops,* Historical Division, Department of the Army, Washington DC, 1947

Konrad F. Schreier. *Tanks & Artillery,* Krause Publications, Iola, 1994

Frank N. Schubert. *The Mobilization,* US Army Center of Military History, Washington DC, 1993

Shelby L. Stanton. *Order of Battle US Army, World War II,* Presidio Press, Novato, California, 1984

Steven J. Zaloga. *US Field Artillery of World War II,* Osprey Publishing Ltd, New York, 2007

Organization and Equipment of the United States Army, War Department, Washington, DC, April 1943.

The Officer's Guide, The Military Service Publishing Company, Harrisburg, Pennsylvania, July 1943 edition.

Aide-mémoire de l'officier d'Etat-major, Centre de formation des officiers d'Etat-major, Rabat, novembre 1943.

Order of Battle of the United States Army, World War II, European Theater of

Operations, Divisions, Office of the Theater Historian, Paris, 1945.

Caractéristiques des principaux matériels d'artillerie américaine, Etat-major Guerre 4e bureau, Paris, 1949,

The Army Almanac, The Stackpole Company, Harrisburg, Pennsylvania, 1959.

Conception & layout: Alexandre Thers and Jean-Marie Mongin. Cover design: Gil Bourdeaux

ISBN: 978-2-35250-058-2
Editor Number: 35250

© Histoire & Collections 2009

5, avenue de la République
F-75541 Paris Cédex 11 — France

Tel: +33 1 40 21 18 20
Fax +33 1 47 00 51 11
www.histoireetcollections.fr

This book has been designed, typed, laid-out and processed by Histoire & Collections, fully on integrated computer equipment

Print run completed in March 2009 on the presses of Elkar-MCC Graphics, Spain, European Union